simple ways to success

healthy

Lesley Waters

photography by Gus Filgate

First published exclusively for J Sainsbury plc in 2003 by Quadrille Publishing Limited
Alhambra House 27-31 Charing Cross Road London WC2H 0LS

Editorial director Jane O'Shea **Creative director** Helen Lewis
Managing editor Janet Illsley **Art direction and design** Vanessa Courtier
Photographer Gus Filgate **Food stylist** Silvana Franco **Props stylist** Jane Campsie
Editor Barbara Croxford **Production** Vincent Smith and Jane Rogers

Cataloguing in Publication Data: a catalogue record for this book is available from the British Library.

ISBN 1 844000 49 4
Printed in China

contents

NOTES

All spoon measures are level unless otherwise stated:
1 teaspoon = 5ml spoon, 1 tablespoon = 15ml spoon.

Use fresh herbs unless dried herbs are suggested.

Use freshly ground black pepper unless otherwise stated.

Free-range eggs are recommended and large eggs should be used
except where a different size is specified.

Recipes which feature raw or lightly cooked eggs should be avoided
by anyone who is pregnant or in a vulnerable health group.

introduction

Whether I am working on television, teaching or writing, I am often asked if it is really possible to deliver simple, tasty, healthy food every day, with the minimum of effort. And my answer is yes, because for me this is what good food is all about. Healthy eating is not a fad, it's not a diet, nor is it something you practice for two weeks before your summer holiday. It's a great way to live and enjoy your food. And that, quite simply, is what this book is all about.

Most of us lead busy lives and time is precious. Finding the time to shop, cook and eat three meals a day without resorting to quick fixes can seem impossible at times, but it can be done. Once hooked on a healthy diet, you will never look back and you will reap the benefits. I believe it is the simple changes that make the difference. It's not about giving up everything that is tasty and good to eat, just about making adjustments.

The key to healthy eating is about making changes that easily become part of your everyday life. One adjustment you can make is to invest in great fresh produce. Ask any top chef and he or she will tell you that to create tasty, simple food, quality is everything. Consider free-range and organic foods, and when it comes to fish and meat I look for the best quality possible, always bearing in mind that less is more and quality counts.

Enjoying your food in the company of others is a great way to socialise with family and friends, and helps children form good eating habits. However hectic your day is, do try to sit down to at least one meal with the family. Take the time to eat slowly and chew your food properly – this makes it easier to digest, and easier for your body to absorb the nutrients. Avoid overeating – recognise when you are full, then stop. Try not to skip meals and you will really look forward to and enjoy the next meal.

This book begins with an introduction to the basic principles, or 'building blocks', that are essential to a good diet. It covers balanced nutrition, judicious shopping, useful equipment, healthy cooking methods and food safety. The recipe chapters that follow provide a wealth of exciting, tasty dishes, based on fresh ingredients and uncomplicated cooking techniques. Every meal occasion is covered, from breakfast, through lunchboxes, tasty snacks, suppers and dinners. Scrumptious puddings are included too, because healthy eating is about a balanced approach to food, not excluding those foods that you enjoy.

For easy reference, the recipes are arranged according to the type of food: fish, chicken and turkey, vegetables and salads, and so forth. Each recipe chapter contains an appropriate feature, which includes several recipe ideas and healthy diet tips. With this innovative easy-to-follow cookbook, you will soon find that healthy eating becomes a positive pleasure.

building blocks

Eating a variety of foods is the key to a nutritious, healthy diet. It's also important to balance your intake. The best diet includes plenty of fresh ingredients, covering the whole range of food types, to ensure your body gets enough of the essential nutrients: proteins, vitamins, minerals, carbohydrates and fats. Some foods are obviously better for you than others – here is a guide.

Hydration

Our bodies are made up of approximately 80% water, so top of my list has to be water. Although it isn't a nutrient, water is vital for so many of our bodily functions. Ideally, we should consume around 2 litres (3½ pints) water a day. That is equivalent to a big bottle of still mineral water or 8 large glasses a day. For many of us, this is difficult to achieve, but other drinks help towards that target (excluding alcohol), and remember that many fruit and vegetables contain lots of water, so it all adds up. Tea and coffee both have a diuretic effect, encouraging the body to eliminate water, so they should be consumed in moderation. Always provide water with meals, and try to remember to drink at least a large glass or two in between meals.

Five-a-day fruit and veg

This is the recommended number of fruit and vegetable portions that we should consume every day. Fruit and vegetables are valuable because they supply the body's defence system with the vitamins, minerals and fibre it needs to keep in good health. 'Five-a-day' may seem a lot, but frozen and canned produce count, as well as dried fruits and fruit juices.

Most vegetables and fruits are virtually fat-free, high in fibre and contain antioxidants. These boost the immune system and may help to protect the body from diseases, including some forms of cancer. Tomatoes, red peppers, mangoes and avocados are particularly high in antioxidants. Vegetables and fruits vary in the essential nutrients that they provide, so you need to eat a good variety for maximum benefit. Fresh vegetables can be cooked in so many interesting ways, or eaten raw in salads or as crudités for dipping. Beyond the fruit bowl, enjoy quick smoothies, fruit salads, salsas, hot fruity puddings, and dried fruit as snacks. Buy good quality fruit juice, or if you have a juicer, make your own delicious vegetable and fruit juices.

Protein foods

We need far less protein than most of us consume – as little as 75g (3oz) a day is generally sufficient. Again, variety is the key. White meat is a good source of protein and it has less saturated fat than red meat, although you can now buy very lean cuts of red meat. Fish is an excellent source of protein, especially oily fish such as salmon, mackerel and sardines. And don't forget beans and lentils, nuts and seeds, which provide valuable vitamins and minerals too. Lastly, there is the versatile egg, a concentrated source of animal protein.

Salt

On average in this country, we consume about 1½ times more salt than is recommended by health professionals. Too much salt can contribute to high blood pressure and has been linked to coronary heart disease, so it makes sense to cut down on your salt intake. These days, I do not use salt in my cooking.

If you wish to add salt to some of these recipes, that's fine, but try to cut down gradually. Perhaps the first step is to stop adding it during cooking. When you are accustomed to the new taste, banish the salt pot from the table. It is amazing how quickly your tastebuds adjust and you find you prefer less salt.

Sugar

Refined sugars provide 'empty calories' and, if eaten frequently, increase the risk of tooth decay, so we should aim to cut down on these. Apart from the obvious sources, like sweets, biscuits and cakes, watch out for hidden sugars in processed foods, such as sweetened breakfast cereals. Try to buy 'no added sugar' breakfast cereals and sweeten with naturally sweet fresh and dried fruits – try sprinkling raisins and fresh banana slices on muesli, for example.

Soft drinks, in particular, can contain large quantities of added sugar. Choose fresh fruit juices without added sugar, and look for lower sugar options if you buy fruit squashes.

Fats

In general, we consume too much fat. A small amount of fat plays an important part in the overall balance of a healthy diet, but eating too much is harmful. Fats are composed of fatty acids, and it is the saturated type found in meat, dairy products and hard cooking fats that are particularly harmful.

A high intake of saturated fatty acids is linked to an increased risk of heart disease, obesity and certain forms of cancer. To cut down, avoid dripping and lard, and be wary of the hidden fats in bought biscuits, cakes, pastries and some ready meals. Opt for lean cuts of meat and smaller portions, topping up your plate with plenty of vegetables. Choose very strong cheese to use in cooking, such as Parmesan, because you'll need only a small amount to impart flavour. And butter? Well it makes sense to cut down, but I prefer a fine scraping of natural butter on toast to any of the low-fat spreads now available. It's all a question of awareness and a balanced approach.

Monounsaturated fatty acids are found in foods such as olive oil, sesame and rapeseed oils, avocados, seeds and most nuts. These are not detrimental to health provided they are consumed in moderation (to avoid weight gain), and they can help to lower the potentially harmful type of cholesterol in blood.

Polyunsaturated fatty acids include the essential omega-3 and omega-6 fatty acids that are important for growth, a healthy skin and a strong immune system. Oily fish, soya beans and rapeseed oil are good sources of omega-3's; vegetable oils, such as sunflower and olive oil, contain omega-6's. These are beneficial sources of fat.

Hydrogenated fats found in cooking fats, margarines, pastries and processed ready meals, contain trans fatty acids which work like saturated fats. It is therefore preferable to avoid these or limit your intake in the same way as saturated fats.

Fibre

This isn't a nutrient as such, but it is an important constituent of food, which helps to keep the digestive system healthy. Wholemeal bread, wholegrain cereals, fruit, vegetables, pulses and nuts are good sources.

my top ten 'super foods'

There are some foods that are so nutritious you could almost call them 'super foods'. These foods contain beneficial oils and/or high levels of antioxidants in the form of beta-carotene and vitamins C and E, all of which contribute to helping to reduce the risk of serious diseases, such as heart disease and certain forms of cancer. Eat them regularly to maximise the benefits to your diet. Many foods could be described as 'super foods', but these are my ten favourites.

Avocado   This fruit is rich in beneficial monounsaturated fatty acids, contains more protein than any other fruit, and is and an excellent source of vitamin E.

Bananas   An excellent instant energy food and easy to digest, bananas are also high in potassium, magnesium and some B vitamins.

Berries   Blackcurrant, blueberries, blackberries and black grapes are all high in antioxidants.

Green vegetables   Brassicas, such as broccoli, Brussels sprouts, cabbage and greens, contain beneficial phytochemicals called indoles, which can help to detoxify the body when eaten regularly. They are also useful sources of minerals.

Oats   Whole grain oats are an excellent source of soluble fibre and a slow-release form of carbohydrate. When eaten as part of a low-fat diet, oats can help to maintain a healthy heart.

Oily fish   All varieties – including salmon, mackerel, tuna, trout and sardines – are good sources of protein and rich in beneficial omega-3 fatty acids, minerals and certain vitamins.

Red and yellow peppers   Rich in beta-carotene and vitamin C.

Seeds   Sesame, pumpkin, and sunflower seeds are packed with protein, high in essential oils, and a valuable source of vitamin E and B vitamins.

Soya   An important high quality vegetable protein food, especially for vegetarians, and a good source of minerals, B vitamins and antioxidants. Soya is available as bean curd (tofu), soya milk, cheese and yogurts.

Tomatoes   Another colourful food that is rich in beta-carotene and a good source of vitamins C and E.

'storecupboard' essentials

Certain ingredients have become the jewels of my kitchen cupboards, fridge and freezer. These items ensure that tasty, healthy food is achievable every single day and I would be lost without them. In addition, I always have a huge bowl of apples, pears, oranges, lemons and limes on the kitchen table, and a bunch of bananas in a separate bowl.

Kitchen cupboards   I keep a selection of the basic grain staples such as pasta, cous cous, cracked wheat, polenta and different rices, plus different coloured lentils, canned beans and tomatoes, and packets of nuts and seeds. For flavouring dishes, my storecupboard jewels are: Thai curry pastes, half-fat coconut milk, wine and balsamic vinegars, soy, teriyaki, Tabasco and Worcestershire sauces, Dijon and wholegrain mustards, chilli flakes and a selection of spices including ground coriander, sweet paprika and garam masala. If you are trying to cut down on salt, these flavourings – together with fresh herbs, ginger and garlic – will give you all the taste you need. You'll also need good quality olive oil to use in moderation for cooking and salad dressings. And for flavouring sweet dishes, you'll find honey, maple syrup and vanilla extract invaluable.

Refrigerator   There is always fresh fruit juice, milk, yogurt, eggs, a piece of strong Cheddar cheese and a wedge of Parmesan in my fridge. Lean back bacon, olive tapenade, sun-blushed tomatoes, tahini and fresh ready-made pesto are there to add flavour to simple staples. In the vegetable drawer, you'll find nutritious broccoli, carrots, peppers and baby spinach leaves. The salad drawer invariably contains a bag of salad leaves, ripe red tomatoes, cucumber and a selection of chillies for easy raitas and spicy salsas.

Freezer   I have never been inclined to cook up meals for the freezer. They lose some qualities on freezing and I prefer to eat dishes at their best. However, I would not be without my freezer-standbys, such as sweetcorn, peas and spinach, red summer fruits and frozen yogurts. A few pitta breads and good quality loaves are always handy for those occasions when you run short.

key cooking methods

Modern cooking equipment greatly increases the options for healthy cooking techniques. Good quality non-stick pans enable you to create appetising, tasty dishes using the minimum of oil or fat. They are important for many of the recipes in this book and essential for methods such as steam-frying. If you do not have them already, invest in a large non-stick wok with a lid, a shallow non-stick frying pan with a lid, one or two non-stick saucepans and non-stick roasting tins in two different sizes. For baking, non-stick muffins tins and good quality non-stick baking trays and baking sheets will make all the difference.

Steaming

Steaming is a classic cooking method for healthy food. Chinese bamboo steamers are an attractive option that can be used for serving the food as well as cooking it. Alternatively, try a metal fan style steamer that opens out to fit the pan, or a special purpose pan with a perforated steamer that fits snugly on top. A tight-fitting lid is essential to trap in the steam. Bring the water to the boil in the base of the pan, then put the food in the steamer and cover tightly. The food cooks in the trapped steam and water-soluble vitamins and minerals are retained. You will need to check the water level every so often, to make sure the pan doesn't boil dry.

Poaching

Poaching is an ideal way to cook delicate foods that are inclined to break easily, such as eggs and fish. Bring the liquid to the boil in the pan, then lower the heat and wait until the surface is barely trembling before you add the food. Poaching is also a good method for foods that are liable to become dry. Chicken breasts, for example, remain succulent if you poach them gently in stock or wine flavoured with herbs and you can reduce the poaching liquor to make a tasty sauce.

Griddling

Traditional cast-iron griddle pans are good for cooking steaks and chops, but otherwise their use is limited and they are heavy to handle. The modern, lightweight, non-stick griddle pan is ideal for cooking meat, fish, vegetables and fruits, even for toasting bread. Griddling is like upside-down grilling, as the heat of the pan sears the food on the outside giving it an inviting appearance, taste and texture, with the added advantage that very little fat is needed. Make sure the griddle pan is really hot before you start. If you need a little oil, this should be brushed on to the food, not the pan. Press down on the food with the back of a fish slice as it cooks to give defined char-grill lines, but don't move it around too much.

Stir-frying

The oriental art of stir-frying is a fast, healthy way of cooking food and nutrients are well retained. Once again you need to start with a hot pan, but this time when the food is added, you need to keep it moving to ensure even cooking. Have all your ingredients ready chopped or sliced to a similar size before you start – once you start you can't stop! Make sure the wok is really hot before you add any ingredients and avoid adding too many items in one go, otherwise you will lower the temperature. Use a large spoon, wooden spatula or fish slice to toss and stir the food constantly.

Steam-frying
I learnt this brilliant way of cooking from a good friend. It is a simple technique that uses the minimum amount of oil, while maximising the flavours in the food. Using a non-stick pan, start to fry the ingredient(s) in a little oil over a medium heat until slightly coloured. Add a tablespoon or so of water and cover immediately with a tight-fitting lid to create steam in the pan. Continue to cook over a low heat. If your lid isn't really tight, cover the food directly with a damp piece of greaseproof paper or baking parchment, then with a lid. Don't keep lifting the lid, as steam will be lost and the pan will dry out. Should this happen, just add a splash more water.

Grilling
Meat, fish and vegetables can all benefit from grilling as it sears the outside of the food, leaving it juicy and succulent within. Preheat the grill to the correct temperature, and keep a close eye on the food as it grills, turning frequently to ensure even cooking. If it appears to be browning too quickly, either move the shelf down or lower the heat.

Oven roasting
This familiar cooking method requires the least effort on the part of the cook. Simply preheat the oven to the right temperature, toss the foods in a roasting tin with a little oil or marinade and place in the oven. The dry heat draws out the juices from the food, concentrating the flavours, and caramelising the surface to delicious effect. You will need to turn or baste the food occasionally during roasting, remembering to shut the oven door as you do so, to keep the oven temperature up. Even vegetables need a little shaking and tossing half way through roasting.

1 breakfasts, snacks and packed lunches

spiked balsamic beef tomatoes with crispy ham

Breakfast with a zing – sizzling tomatoes with an extra bite of chilli and piquant balsamic vinegar to get you started. If you don't fancy chilli in the morning, try scattering the tomatoes with a little shredded fresh basil instead, or omit the balsamic vinegar and sprinkle over the more traditional Worcestershire sauce if you like. Tomatoes are a great source of vitamins A and C.

SERVES 4

4 beefsteak tomatoes, halved
1 teaspoon dried chilli flakes
1 teaspoon caster sugar
1¹/₂ tablespoons olive oil
70g packet Parma or Black Forest ham
balsamic vinegar, to drizzle
freshly ground black pepper
basil leaves, to serve (optional)

1 Preheat the oven to 200°C (fan oven 180°C), gas mark 6. Place the tomatoes, cut-side up, on a non-stick baking tray. Mix together the chilli, sugar and olive oil, then drizzle over the tomato halves. Grind over plenty of black pepper. Bake for 12–15 minutes until the tomatoes are cooked through but still keeping their shape.

2 Meanwhile, grill the ham for 1 minute each side or until crispy. Place the tomatoes on four warm serving plates, then drizzle each with a little balsamic vinegar. Top with the crispy ham, scatter with basil leaves if you like and serve, with Granary toast.

apricot and maple muffins

Even with added fibre-rich bran, these fruity muffins remain beautifully moist. They are flavoured with dried apricots, one of the best sources of iron and potassium, and sweetened with maple syrup. Great for breakfast on the go, or simply pack them into lunchboxes.

MAKES 8–10

2 eggs
250ml (8fl oz) semi-skimmed milk
2 tablespoons olive oil
3 tablespoons natural yogurt
50g (2oz) All-bran

225g (8oz) plain white flour
1 tablespoon baking powder
25g (1oz) light muscovado sugar
125g (4oz) dried apricots, chopped
50g (2oz) sultanas
2 tablespoons maple syrup

  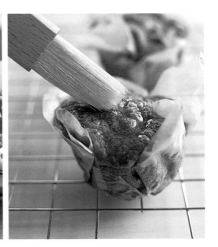

1 Preheat the oven to 190°C (fan oven 170°C), gas mark 5. Line a large muffin tin with 8–10 paper cases or greaseproof paper. In a measuring jug, mix together the eggs, milk, olive oil, yogurt and bran. Set aside.

2 Sift the flour and baking powder into a bowl, then stir in the sugar, dried apricots and sultanas. Add the egg mixture and mix well until smooth. Spoon the mixture into the muffin cases.

3 Bake for 15–20 minutes until golden and cooked through. Insert a skewer into the middle of one muffin to test – when cooked, the skewer will come out clean. Remove from the oven.

4 Allow the muffins to cool in the tin for a couple of minutes, then transfer to a wire rack and brush with the maple syrup. Serve warm or at room temperature.

banana breakfast bread

A simple, quick bread that oozes with hot honeyed bananas. Bananas are a good source of vitamin B6, which is said to fight off viruses, plus vitamin C and magnesium. They're an ideal fruit to eat between meals, to give you that energy burst you sometimes need during the day.

MAKES 9 LARGE BUNS
290g packet pizza dough mix
3 medium bananas, peeled
grated zest of 1 orange
1 tablespoon poppy seeds
1/2 teaspoon ground cinnamon
1 1/2 tablespoons thin honey

1 Preheat the oven to 200°C (fan oven 180°C), gas mark 6. Lightly oil a 20cm (8 inch) square non-stick baking tin. Make up the dough mix according to the packet instructions. Roll out to a rectangle, approximately 30x25cm (12x10 inches).

2 Slice the bananas and place in a bowl with the orange zest, poppy seeds, cinnamon and half of the honey. Toss to mix, then spoon the mixture over the dough, leaving a 1cm (1/2 inch) border.

3 Roll up the dough from a long side and press the edges together to seal. Cut into nine equal pieces and place the dough pieces, cut-side up, in the tin.

4 Bake for 15–20 minutes. Warm the remaining honey in the microwave for 5 seconds (or in a small pan) and brush over the breakfast bread. Leave in the tin to cool slightly, then remove. Pull the buns apart to serve – they are best eaten warm.

tea scented warm fruits

This simple dried fruit compote is perfect served with hot porridge, breakfast wheat flakes or simply on its own. As well as being full of fibre, dried fruits are a good source of iron. Other varieties can be substituted, such as ready-to-eat dried apricots, if you prefer.

SERVES 4
150g (5oz) dried figs
150g (5oz) ready-to-eat prunes
150g (5oz) dried pears
2 sachets lemon green tea
1 tablespoon thin honey

1 Put the dried figs, prunes and pears into a saucepan. Add the tea bags, 600ml (1 pint) water and the honey. Bring to the boil, lower the heat and simmer for 10 minutes.

2 Remove the tea bags and tip the fruits and syrup into a non-metallic bowl. Serve warm, or set aside to cool then cover and refrigerate until needed.

oaty orange and fig pots

There's nothing like porridge oats to set you up for the day. Oats are good for your heart as they help reduce cholesterol, and they encourage the digestive system to run smoothly. Here orange juice and chopped figs provide an added kick of vitamin C and fibre.

SERVES 2
125g (4oz) large oats
4 dried figs, roughly chopped, or a generous
   handful of sultanas or raisins
300ml (1/2 pint) orange juice
TO SERVE:
Greek yogurt
toasted flaked almonds (optional)

1 Divide the oats and dried fruit between two serving bowls and pour over the orange juice. Cover and chill for 4 hours or overnight.

2 To serve, top each portion with a spoonful of yogurt and sprinkle with toasted almonds if you like.

a healthy start

Breakfast is a meal that is often ignored or overlooked, or deliberately skipped, either through lack of time or interest, or in the mistaken belief that it will help weight loss. A tasty, nourishing breakfast will set you up for the day, getting your body working better and your brain moving faster. Slow release carbohydrates, like oats and bran, are perfect for keeping you going through a busy day, so you won't start to feel hungry mid-morning.

If your mornings are always a frantic rush (with everyone fighting for the bathroom), breakfast in a glass may be more suited to your weekdays or, for the earlier risers, pancakes or eggs might just tempt you to the table. Either way it doesn't have to be a huge meal, just a tasty plate, bowl or glassful to give you the best start to the day. Set your alarm in time – you'll be glad you did! Each of the following healthy breakfasts serves 4.

▲ **toasted breakfast wraps**
Chop 2 large bananas and 2 nectarines; toss with 2 tsp thin honey. Heat a non-stick griddle pan over a medium heat. Spoon the fruit down the centre of 4 flour tortillas and roll up, folding in the ends to form wraps. Place seam-side down in the pan and cook for 2 minutes each side. Serve warm.

Alternatively, fill tortillas with scrambled eggs made with 4 eggs, 125g (4oz) honey roast ham slivers and 75g (3oz) halved cherry tomatoes. Cook as above.

posh porridge

Make porridge with jumbo oats according to the packet instructions, using half semi-skimmed milk and half water. Top with a spoonful of natural bio yogurt, chopped dried figs and toasted flaked almonds. For a refreshing summer option, top the porridge with blueberries and a drizzle of maple syrup.

breakfast blinis

Sift 125g (4oz) self-raising flour and ½ tsp ground cinnamon into a bowl. Stir in 15g (½oz) caster sugar, the grated zest of 1 orange and 50g (2oz) sultanas. Make a well in the centre. Beat 1 egg with 200ml (7fl oz) milk and pour into the well. Stir to combine and form a smooth batter. Stir in 50g (2oz) crumbled bran flakes. Heat a large non-stick frying pan. Drop tablespoonfuls of the batter into the pan, spacing apart, and cook for 2 minutes each side until set and golden. Serve warm.

▲ steam-fried eggs

Heat a large, non-stick frying pan until very hot, then carefully wipe with kitchen paper dipped in olive oil. Crack 4 eggs into the pan and reduce the heat to low. Cover, so they start to steam, and cook for about 4 minutes for soft eggs, or flip over for a firm set yolk. Season with black pepper, scatter over a little torn basil and serve on toast. For a spicy variation, flavour with a dash of green Tabasco and scatter with torn coriander.

mango and banana smoothie

A healthy drink is a great start to the morning and with a smoothie you can increase your fruit and fibre intake at a flick of a switch! Make sure the fruit is really ripe, otherwise the consistency and natural sweetness won't be quite right.
Illustrated on previous page

SERVES 2–4
1 large ripe banana, peeled and roughly chopped
1 large ripe mango, peeled, stoned and sliced

grated zest and juice of 1 lime
200ml (7 fl oz) orange juice, or more to taste

1 Place the banana, mango, lime zest and juice, and orange juice in a blender. Blend until smooth, adding more orange juice if required to obtain the desired consistency. Pour into two large glasses or several smaller ones and serve straightaway.

pineapple and passion slush

Creamy and refreshing in one hit – a great start to the morning, or to enjoy at any time as one of your five-a-day fruit and veg. Be sure to buy pineapple canned in its own juice, rather than heavy syrup.

SERVES 4
430g can pineapple slices, in natural juice

300g natural bio fat-free yogurt
1 passion fruit, halved

1 Place the pineapple slices and juice in a blender with the yogurt. Put 10 ice cubes into a plastic bag and bash with a rolling pin to crush lightly. Tip the ice into the blender and whiz until frothy and just smooth. Pour the drink into four glasses and spoon a little passion fruit pulp on top to serve.

pink panther

This delicious drink provides a real burst of energy in a glass and boosts your vitamin C intake. For a summer cooler, replace the vanilla yogurt with frozen vanilla yogurt.

SERVES 2–4
175g (6 oz) mixed strawberries and raspberries

150ml (¼ pint) cranberry juice
225g (8 oz) low-fat vanilla yogurt

1 Place the strawberries, raspberries, cranberry juice and vanilla yogurt in a blender and whiz until smooth. Fill two large glasses or several smaller tumblers with crushed ice and pour the smoothie on top to serve.

chunky pear and vanilla flapjacks

These crumbly, fruity flapjacks are high in fibre and low in fat. Packed with cranberries and pears, they make a great lunchbox filler, or snack at any time of the day. Buy pure vanilla extract rather than essence – it has a far superior flavour.

MAKES 10
7 tablespoons thin honey
3 teaspoons vanilla extract
150g (5oz) porridge oats
75g (3oz) dried cranberries
2 medium ripe pears, peeled, cored and chopped

1 Preheat the oven to 180°C (fan oven 160°C), gas mark 4. Heat the honey in a saucepan, add the vanilla, then stir in the oats, cranberries and pears.

2 Press the mixture into an 18cm (7 inch) square non-stick baking tin and bake for 20 minutes. Leave to cool in the tin for 10 minutes, then mark into 10 bars and leave to cool completely before removing.

sultana and cranberry rockies

These quick and easy, sustaining treats are best eaten on the day they are made. Dried cranberries are widely available now and lend a tangy, sweet flavour.

MAKES 8
25g (1oz) unsalted butter
125g (4oz) self-raising flour
40g (1½oz) muscovado sugar
25g (1oz) sultanas
25g (1oz) dried cranberries
1 egg, beaten
1 tablespoon milk

1 Preheat the oven to 180°C (fan oven 160°C), gas mark 4. Lightly oil a non-stick baking sheet. Put the butter and flour into a mixing bowl and rub together with your fingertips until the mixture resembles fine breadcrumbs. Stir in the sugar, sultanas and cranberries. Mix in the egg and milk to form a soft dough.

2 Drop spoonfuls of the mixture on to the baking sheet, spacing out well. Bake for 12–15 minutes until golden. Transfer to a wire rack to cool.

mango and carrot crumble cookies

Crumbly around the edges and moist in the middle, these cookies are a great favourite with my children. The grated fresh carrot and dried mango lend sweetness and plenty of goodness. Porridge oats provide crunch and soluble fibre which, when eaten as part of a low-fat diet, can help maintain a healthy heart.

MAKES 16

50g (2oz) butter
65g (2½oz) dark muscovado sugar
1 egg
50g (2oz) plain flour

½ teaspoon bicarbonate of soda
150g (5oz) porridge oats
1 small carrot, peeled and grated
65g (2½oz) dried mango, finely chopped

1 Preheat the oven to 190°C (fan oven 170°C), gas mark 5. In a large bowl, cream the butter and sugar together. Add the egg and beat until well mixed.

2 Sift the flour and bicarbonate of soda together over the mixture, then add the porridge oats, grated carrot and chopped mango. Fold in, using a large metal spoon, until evenly mixed.

3 Drop tablespoons of the dough on to a non-stick baking sheet and press down gently. Bake for 15–20 minutes or until lightly golden around the edges.

4 Leave the cookies on the baking sheet for a few minutes, then transfer to a wire rack to cool.

butter bean houmous

This really creamy, protein-rich houmous is so easy to make. Provide a colourful selection of vegetables for dipping, such as carrot and celery sticks, cherry tomatoes, crunchy radishes and little lettuce hearts. There's no need to cook dried chick peas – you'll find a good selection of organic canned beans on the shelves. Tahini is made from sesame seeds, which provide the body with calcium, good for strong bones and teeth. It can be found in the special selection range.

SERVES 4

400g can butter beans, drained and rinsed
400g can chick peas, drained and rinsed
2 garlic cloves, peeled and crushed
2 tablespoon tahini
3 tablespoons extra virgin olive oil
3 tablespoons natural yogurt
juice of 1/2 lemon
sea salt and freshly ground black pepper

1 Put the butter beans, chick peas, garlic, tahini, olive oil, yogurt and lemon juice in a food processor and add about 5 tablespoons cold water. Blend until just smooth.

2 Season the houmous with a little sea salt and pepper to taste. Transfer to a bowl or plastic tub and serve with vegetable dippers and pitta bread strips.

tuna pan bagna

This is a crusty roll filled to the brim with juicy semi-dried tomatoes, crispy leaves, tuna and a creamy dressing. Semi-dried or sunblush tomatoes can be found on the deli counter. Canned tuna is high in protein and vitamins, but unfortunately it is not a good source of the omega-3 essential fatty acids because most of these are lost in the canning process.

MAKES 4

4 ciabatta rolls
6 tablespoons natural yogurt
1 garlic clove, peeled and crushed
1 teaspoon lemon juice
100g (3½oz) sunblush tomatoes
50g (2oz) crisp salad leaves
2 x 160g cans yellow fin tuna in spring water,
  drained
1 punnet mustard and cress, trimmed
freshly ground black pepper

1   Cut the top off each roll to make a lid. Hollow out the centre of the rolls. (Use the bread that you remove to make breadcrumbs and freeze until needed.)

2   To make the dressing, whisk the yogurt, garlic and lemon juice together in a bowl, then season with pepper to taste.

3   Spoon the sunblush tomatoes into the ciabatta cavities and cover with a layer of salad leaves. Spoon on some of the yogurt dressing, then add the tuna, more dressing and a final layer of mustard and cress, pressing down lightly as you fill the rolls.

4   Place the lids on top to enclose the filling and press lightly. Wrap the rolls in greaseproof paper and refrigerate or keep in a chilled insulated lunchbox for a few hours before eating (no longer or they may become a little soggy).

pesto picnic pasta

This nutritious salad is ideal to pack into tubs for lunchboxes. The pasta soaks up all the lovely flavours of the basil pesto and marries well with tender chicken, juicy tomatoes and cucumber.

SERVES 4–6

200g (7oz) dried pasta shapes, such as penne
* or shells*
3 tablespoons ready-made fresh pesto sauce
2 tablespoons extra virgin olive oil
150g (5oz) cooked chicken breast, shredded
250g (9oz) cherry tomatoes, halved
1 cucumber, peeled, deseeded and chopped
freshly ground black pepper

1 Cook the pasta in a large pan of boiling water, according to the packet instructions, until *al dente* (tender, but firm to the bite). Drain and rinse under cold water to stop further cooking, then place in a large bowl and set aside to cool completely.

2 Meanwhile, for the dressing, whisk the pesto and olive oil together in a large mixing bowl. Season with pepper to taste.

3 Add the pasta, chicken, tomatoes and cucumber to the pesto dressing and toss well together. Transfer the pasta salad to a lidded container and refrigerate or keep in a chilled lunchbox until needed.

2 soups

green macaroni minestrone

A twist on the classic minestrone, this fresh-tasting soup is full of vegetables, rich in fibre and very satisfying – a real meal in itself. Enhanced with fresh tomatoes and basil, and drizzled with the finest olive oil, it is best served simply with good crusty bread.

SERVES 4

150ml (¼ pint) white wine
1 onion, peeled and finely chopped
1 garlic clove, peeled and crushed
1.5 litres (2½ pints) vegetable stock
100g (3½oz) macaroni
125g (4oz) French beans, trimmed and cut into
  2.5cm (1 inch) lengths
400g can cannellini beans, drained and rinsed
75g (3oz) frozen petit pois
2 ripe tomatoes, chopped
3 tablespoons chopped basil
freshly ground black pepper
4 teaspoons extra virgin olive oil, to serve

1   Pour the white wine into a large pan and add the onion and garlic. Cover the pan and steam-fry for 6 minutes or until softened, stirring occasionally.

2   Add the stock and bring to the boil. Tip in the macaroni and cook for 6 minutes. Stir in the French beans and simmer for 3 minutes, then add cannellini beans and petit pois and simmer for a further 2 minutes.

3   Add the tomatoes and basil, and heat through for 1 minute. Season well with pepper. Ladle the minestrone into four warm bowls and drizzle each with a teaspoon of extra virgin olive oil to serve.

veggie barley broth with garlic toasts

This hearty broth of root vegetables is full of fibre, which helps the body to absorb nutrients. It is thickened with pearl barley, which may sound rather old-fashioned but it is an excellent grain and very under-rated. It has a lovely, nutty flavour and a wonderful, almost creamy texture in soups and stews.

SERVES 4

1.5 litres (2½ pints) chicken or vegetable stock
100g (3½oz) pearl barley
1 leek, trimmed
2 celery sticks
2 large carrots, peeled
1 medium parsnip, peeled
5 tablespoons white wine

2 tablespoons sun-dried tomato purée
2 bay leaves
2 tablespoons chopped parsley
freshly ground black pepper

FOR THE GARLIC TOASTS:
1 rustic loaf, sliced
1 garlic clove, peeled and halved

1 Pour the stock into a pan, add the pearl barley and boil gently for 10 minutes. Meanwhile, finely chop the leek, celery, carrots and parsnip.

2 Pour the wine into a large pan, add the leek, cover and steam-fry for 5 minutes, stirring occasionally. Add the remaining vegetables and cook for a further 5 minutes.

3 Stir in the tomato purée, bay leaves, pearl barley and stock. Bring to the boil, lower the heat and simmer for 15–20 minutes.

4 Meanwhile, toast the bread on both sides, then rub with the garlic clove. Season the soup with pepper to taste and stir in the parsley. Pour into warm bowls and serve with the garlic toasts.

spiced red lentil and sweet potato soup

Quick cooking red lentils and sweet potato cubes are spiced with medium or mild curry paste, then mellowed with reduced-fat coconut milk to make a comforting, warming soup. Lentils are full of fibre which aids digestion, they are also a good source of vegetable protein. Serve this rich-textured soup with warm chapatti bread as a lunch or light supper.

SERVES 4

350g (12oz) potatoes
1 large sweet potato
2 tablespoons ready-made curry paste, such as
 Madras or korma
1 onion, peeled and finely chopped
125g (4oz) split red lentils
900ml (1½ pints) vegetable stock
200ml (7fl oz) reduced-fat coconut milk
1–2 tablespoons chopped coriander leaves, plus
 sprigs to garnish
freshly ground black pepper
chapatti breads, to serve

1 Peel the potatoes and sweet potato and cut into 1cm (½ inch) cubes. Heat the curry paste in a pan, stir in the onion, cover and steam-fry for 5 minutes, stirring occasionally.

2 Add the potatoes, sweet potato, lentils and stock to the pan. Bring to the boil, then lower the heat and simmer for 20 minutes.

3 Stir in the coconut milk and gently heat through. Season to taste with pepper, then stir in the chopped coriander. Ladle the soup into warm bowls, top with coriander sprigs and serve with warm chapatti breads.

speedy soups

You can create tempting, flavourful soups without resorting to boiling up carcasses in the stockpot. Use aromatics like ginger, lemon grass and chillies for an oriental style pot, or try infusing water or light vegetable stock with sweet root vegetables, such as carrot, parsnip and leek. Soups that are bursting with vegetables will only need plain water. For an instant gentle stock, save your vegetable cooking water.

Ready-made fresh stocks are available from the chilled cabinet, or you can buy stocks in cube or powdered form. Seek out quality dried stock products, especially salt-free products. Dried stocks can be strong, so dilute with plenty of water. Toss in a few simple ingredients, such as chilli, noodles and prawns, or curry paste, chicken and spinach, to transform your stock into a bowl of steaming goodness. Each of the following soups serves 4 as a starter, or light meal accompanied with bread.

▲ garlic mussel bisque

Heat 1 tbsp olive oil in a large pan, stir in 3 crushed garlic cloves and cook for 30 seconds. Add 850g (1lb 14oz) cleaned, scrubbed, closed mussels, 350g pot fresh arrabiatta sauce and 300ml (½ pint) red wine. Cover with a lid and cook for 2–3 minutes or until the mussels have opened; discard any that remain closed. Ladle into serving bowls, scatter over chopped parsley and serve straightaway with crusty, country bread.

curried chicken soup

Heat 2 tbsp ready-made curry paste in a pan, then add 1 thinly sliced onion. Cover and cook for 5 minutes, stirring occasionally. Add 250g (9oz) chicken breast fillet, cut into thin strips, and cook for 1 minute. Add 1 litre (1¾ pints) chicken stock, bring to the boil and simmer for 5 minutes. Stir in 175g (6oz) baby leaf spinach and 2 tbsp mango chutney. Heat through and season with pepper. Serve with warm chapattis.

hot and sour soup

Heat 1 tsp groundnut oil in a pan, and stir in ½ tsp dried red chilli flakes, 2.5cm (1 inch) finely chopped fresh root ginger and 1 crushed garlic clove. Cook for 1 minute. Add 1.2 litres (2 pints) chicken stock and simmer gently for 10 minutes. Stir in 250g (9oz) peeled, raw tiger prawns, 1 tbsp Thai fish sauce, 150g (5oz) halved sugar snap peas, 125g (4oz) rice noodles and the juice and grated zest of 1 lime. Bring to the boil and simmer for 3 minutes. Serve at once.

▲ pea and basil soup with tomato bruschetta

Cook 1 chopped onion in 1 tsp olive oil in a covered pan for 8 minutes; stir occasionally. Add 1 litre (1¾ pints) vegetable stock and 500g (1lb 2oz) petit pois. Bring to the boil, then simmer for 3 minutes. Whiz in a blender until smooth, then reheat, stirring in 3 tbsp ready-made fresh pesto. Season with pepper. Serve with thick slices of toasted ciabatta, rubbed with garlic and topped with chopped tomatoes and a drizzle of extra virgin olive oil.

portobello mushroom and bacon soup

This wonderful, dark soup is intensely flavoured with portobello mushrooms and thickened with a little brown bread. If you cannot obtain portobello mushrooms, use large field mushrooms instead. Mushrooms are rich in protein and contain B vitamins and useful minerals, and they are very low in calories provided you fry them in the minimum of oil. The soup is finished with a tasty topping of grilled whole mushrooms and crispy Parma ham.
Illustrated on previous page

SERVES 4

500g (1lb 2oz) portobello mushrooms, plus
    4 whole ones to serve
3 teaspoons olive oil
1 onion, peeled and finely chopped
1 garlic clove, peeled and crushed
1 litre (1³/4 pints) vegetable stock
2 small slices of brown bread, crusts removed
3 tablespoons half-fat crème fraîche
4 slices of Parma ham
1 tablespoon snipped chives
freshly ground black pepper

1 Peel the portobello mushrooms, set aside the 4 whole ones for serving and slice the rest. Heat 2 teaspoons of the olive oil in a large pan. Add the onion and garlic, cover and cook for 8 minutes or until soft, stirring occasionally.

2 Stir in the sliced mushrooms and cook for 4 minutes. Add the stock and bring to the boil. Lower the heat and simmer for 10 minutes. Add the bread to the pan and simmer for a further 5 minutes.

3 Pour the soup into a blender and whiz until smooth. Return to the pan, place over a low heat and stir in the crème fraîche. Season well with pepper.

4 Meanwhile, preheat the grill. Place the 4 whole mushrooms, cup-side up, on a baking tray. Drizzle with the remaining olive oil and grind over black pepper. Grill for 3 minutes. Lay the Parma ham on the tray alongside the mushrooms and grill for a further 1 minute or until crispy.

5 Pour the hot soup into warm bowls and top each serving with a grilled mushroom, crispy Parma ham and snipped chives.

Moorish prawn and chick pea soup

Inspired by Middle Eastern flavours, this is a great storecupboard recipe that uses canned chick peas and tomatoes. Tomatoes contain lycopene, which is thought to help reduce the risk of certain cancers. Regular eating of fresh or processed tomatoes is said to lessen the risk of heart disease, and bowel and prostate cancers. To serve, the soup is topped with fragrant cous cous, flavoured with lemon, coriander and prawns.

SERVES 4

100g (3¹/₂oz) cous cous
500g carton passata
400g can chopped tomatoes with garlic
2 teaspoons harissa paste
150ml (¹/₄ pint) white wine
400g can chick peas, drained and rinsed
pinch of sugar
grated zest and juice of ¹/₂ lemon
2 tablespoons extra virgin olive oil
150g (5oz) cooked, peeled prawns
2 tablespoons chopped coriander leaves
freshly ground black pepper

1 Put the cous cous into a bowl, pour over 150ml (¹/₄ pint) boiling water and set aside to soak for 5 minutes until the water is absorbed.

2 Meanwhile, pour the passata and chopped tomatoes into a pan and add the harissa paste and wine. Stir in the chick peas and heat gently for 5 minutes. Season to taste with black pepper and a pinch of sugar.

3 Fluff up the cous cous with a fork. Add the lemon zest and juice, olive oil, prawns and coriander and toss to mix. Season with pepper to taste.

4 Pour the spicy tomato soup into four warm bowls, top with the cous cous and serve straightaway.

smoked fish chowder

A thick, chunky soup made with naturally smoked haddock or cod, potatoes and sweetcorn. Smoked haddock is full of flavour and protein, yet it's very low in fat. Blitzing half the potatoes with the stock and milk gives the chowder a lovely creamy texture without the addition of cream.

SERVES 4

2 teaspoons olive oil
1 onion, peeled and finely chopped
500g (1lb 2oz) potatoes, peeled and diced
600ml (1 pint) fish stock
300ml (½ pint) semi-skimmed milk

340g can sweetcorn in water, drained
450g (1lb) boneless, skinless natural smoked
  haddock or cod, cut into bite-sized pieces
2 tablespoons chopped parsley
freshly ground black pepper

1 Heat the olive oil in a large pan, add the onion and cook for 5 minutes. Add the diced potatoes and cook for a further minute. Pour in the stock and bring to the boil. Lower the heat, cover and simmer for 12–15 minutes or until the potatoes are tender.

2 With a slotted spoon, remove half the potatoes from the stock and set aside. Pour the remaining soup into a blender, add the milk and whiz until smooth. Pour back into the pan.

3 Add the sweetcorn and simmer for 2 minutes. Stir in the fish pieces and reserved potatoes, and cook for a further 3–4 minutes. Stir in the chopped parsley and season with black pepper to taste. Ladle into four warm bowls and serve.

oodles of noodles soup

Rice noodles and chicken soak up all the fragrant oriental flavours in this simple broth. Miso is a traditional Japanese food that is made from fermented soya beans. It is widely available in sachet form; for the stock base, use two or more sachets to taste. Miso is rich in iron, while chicken is an excellent source of easily digestible protein.

SERVES 4

1.2 litres (2 pints) miso broth
1 tablespoon grated fresh root ginger
2 tablespoons good quality soy sauce
250g (9oz) boneless, skinless chicken breast, cut
  into thin strips
125g (4oz) Thai stir-fry rice noodles
200g (7oz) pak choi, divided into leaves
1/2 bunch of spring onions, chopped
2 teaspoons sesame oil
freshly ground black pepper

1 Make up the miso broth according to the packet instructions. Pour into a large pan and add the ginger, soy sauce and chicken strips. Bring to the boil and simmer for 3 minutes.

2 Add the rice noodles and cook for 1 minute. Add the pak choi and cook for a further 1 minute. Stir in the spring onions and simmer for a final minute. Stir in the sesame oil, season with black pepper and serve in warm bowls.

roasted courgette and garlic soup

Roasting vegetables brings out their natural sweetness as they slowly caramelise in the oven and enhances the flavour of soups such as this. Courgettes are a good source of magnesium, which helps the body absorb other important minerals. Half-fat crème fraîche gives the soup a lovely creamy texture, while olive flavoured croûtons provide a crunchy contrast.

SERVES 4

900g (2lb) courgettes, topped and tailed
1 onion, peeled and cut into 8 wedges
3 garlic cloves (unpeeled)
1 tablespoon olive oil
1.2 litres (2 pints) vegetable stock
125g (4oz) frozen petit pois
1 black olive ciabatta
3 tablespoons half-fat crème fraîche
freshly ground black pepper

1 Preheat the oven to 200°C (fan oven 180°C), gas mark 6. Thickly slice the courgettes into 2.5cm (1 inch) chunks.

2 Place the courgettes, onion and garlic in a roasting tin and toss with the olive oil. Season with pepper and roast for 30–35 minutes or until golden and tender.

3 Pour the stock into a saucepan and bring to the boil. Add the petit pois, bring back to the boil, then lower the heat and simmer for 2 minutes until tender.

4 Remove the vegetables from the oven, then peel the garlic cloves. Transfer the roasted vegetables and garlic to a food processor or blender, add the stock and petit pois, and blend until smooth. (It may be necessary to purée the soup in batches.) Season with pepper to taste.

5 Cut the ciabatta into rough 2.5cm (1 inch) cubes and place on a baking tray. Toast in the oven for 5 minutes or until crisp. Meanwhile, pour the soup into the saucepan, stir in the crème fraîche and heat gently. Ladle the soup into warm bowls and serve with the croûtons.

gazpacho with lemon feta bulghar wheat

This easy Mediterranean chilled soup is perfect for a summer lunch. Vitamin B-rich bulghar wheat has a good crunchy texture and needs to be soaked like cous cous. Feta cheese is normally made from sheep's milk and has a distinctive tang. It is a good source of calcium. Together the wheat and feta provide an original topping for the soup.

SERVES 4

400g can chopped tomatoes
300ml (1/2 pint) tomato juice
2 garlic cloves, peeled and crushed
1 tablespoon olive oil
2 tablespoons white wine vinegar
dash of Tabasco sauce
1 red pepper, halved, deseeded and finely diced
100g (3 1/2 oz) bulghar wheat
grated zest and juice of 1/2 lemon
75g (3oz) feta cheese, crumbled
2 tablespoons chopped parsley
freshly ground black pepper

1   Place the chopped tomatoes, tomato juice, garlic, olive oil, wine vinegar and Tabasco in a food processor. Process until smooth and season to taste with black pepper. Stir in the red pepper. Chill the soup for 15 minutes or longer.

2   Tip the bulghar wheat into a bowl, pour over 100ml (3 1/2 fl oz) boiling water and set aside to soak for 10 minutes. Fork through the bulghar wheat and stir in the lemon zest and juice, feta and parsley. Season with pepper to taste.

3   Ladle the chilled soup into individual bowls. Just before serving, top each portion with a spoonful of lemon and feta bulghar wheat.

3 fish

lemon and bay scented hoki with piquant mash

Hoki is a firm white fish from New Zealand, similar to haddock or cod. Simply bake the fish in the oven and infuse it with aromatic bay and vermouth, or use white wine or even fish stock. A great way to make creamy and tasty mash, without adding lashings of butter and cream, is to stir in mustard and natural yogurt.

SERVES 4

4 skinless hoki or haddock fillets, each about
    150g (5oz)
8 bay leaves
1 unwaxed lemon, thinly sliced
4 tablespoons dry vermouth
freshly ground black pepper

FOR THE MASH:
900g (2lb) potatoes, peeled
4 tablespoons natural yogurt
3 tablespoons warm milk
2 tablespoons wholegrain mustard

1 For the mash, cut the potatoes into even-sized chunks and place in a pan of cold water. Bring to the boil, lower the heat and simmer for 20 minutes or until tender. Preheat the oven to 190°C (fan oven 170°C), gas mark 5.

2 Meanwhile, arrange the hoki or haddock fillets in an ovenproof dish and season with black pepper. Place 2 bay leaves on each fish fillet and cover with slices of lemon. Drizzle over the vermouth and cover with damp greaseproof paper. Bake for 10–12 minutes or until the fish is just opaque.

3 Drain the potatoes well and tip back into the pan. Mash over a gentle heat until smooth. Stir in the yogurt, milk and mustard, then season to taste.

4 Serve the hoki with the mustard flavoured mash, and sugar snap peas or mangetout.

mustard crusted cod with caramelised peppers and beans

Cod steaks keep wonderfully moist underneath an unusual crisp topping of cous cous, which is pre-soaked in cold rather than hot water for extra crunch. Red peppers and runner beans provide colour and plenty of vitamin C.

SERVES 4

75g (3oz) cous cous

2 tablespoons Dijon mustard

4 cod steaks, each about 150g (5oz)

3 red peppers

1 tablespoon olive oil

350g (12oz) runner beans, trimmed and sliced

squeeze of lemon juice

freshly ground black pepper

1 Preheat the oven to 200°C (fan oven 180°C), gas mark 6. Place the cous cous in a small bowl, pour over 100ml (3½fl oz) cold water and leave to soak for 5 minutes.

2 Halve, core and deseed the peppers, then cut each half into 4 strips. Place the red peppers in a roasting tray, drizzle over the olive oil and toss well to coat in the oil. Roast for 25–30 minutes.

3 Spread the mustard evenly over the cod steaks, sprinkle the cous cous on top and press to adhere. Set to one side.

4 Toss the green beans in with the peppers and season with black pepper. Sit the cod steaks on top, cous cous side up, and squeeze over the lemon juice. Roast for 8–10 minutes.

5 Meanwhile, preheat the grill. Flash the roasting tin under the grill for 1–2 minutes or until the cous cous crust is golden. Serve immediately.

Parma roasted cod with bean and rocket salad

I find Parma ham and meaty fish work so well together, as their flavours really complement each other. Garlic and lemon enhance the flavour of the flageolet beans, and fresh rocket provides a delicious, peppery contrast.

SERVES 4

4 boneless, skinless cod loins, each about
  150g (5oz)
12 sage leaves
4 slices of Parma ham
2 x 300g cans flageolet beans, drained
  and rinsed
2 garlic cloves, peeled and crushed
2 tablespoons extra virgin olive oil
1 tablespoon lemon juice
125g (4oz) rocket leaves
freshly ground black pepper

1 Preheat the oven to 220°C (fan oven 200°C), gas mark 7. Season the cod with black pepper. Arrange 3 sage leaves on each cod fillet and wrap in a slice of Parma ham. Place in a roasting tin and roast for 6–8 minutes, depending on the thickness of the cod.

2 In the meantime, tip the flageolet beans into a pan. Add the garlic and stir over a medium heat for 2 minutes or until heated through. Add the olive oil and lemon juice and season well. Add the rocket leaves and stir through the beans.

3 Divide the bean and rocket salad between four serving plates and place a portion of roasted Parma-wrapped cod alongside. Serve straightaway.

prawn red Thai noodles

Rice noodles are a lighter alternative to the more familiar Chinese egg noodles. Here they are combined with juicy tiger prawns and crunchy vegetables for a tempting stir-fry that can be made in less time than it takes to pick up the phone and order a takeaway. Peeled raw tiger prawns are available from the freezer cabinet or fresh fish counter. You can also buy whole tiger prawns from selected stores. To prepare these, simply twist off the head and tail, peel away the shell from the body and prise out the dark intestinal vein.

Illustrated on previous page

SERVES 4

1½ tablespoons Thai red curry paste
4 tablespoons passata
125g (4oz) Thai rice noodles
225g (8oz) raw tiger prawns, peeled and
  deveined
200g (7oz) sugar snap peas, halved lengthways
150g (5oz) bean sprouts
50g (2oz) cashew nuts, toasted
lime wedges, to serve

1 Mix the Thai red curry paste and passata together in a small bowl and set aside. Cook the rice noodles according to the packet instructions and drain.

2 Meanwhile, heat a non-stick wok until very hot, then add the peeled tiger prawns and cook for 1 minute. Add half the red Thai paste mix and stir-fry for a further minute. Add the sugar snap peas with 2 tablespoons water and stir-fry for 2 minutes.

3 Stir in the rice noodles, bean sprouts, cashew nuts and remaining red Thai paste mix. Toss over a high heat for a further 2 minutes until piping hot. Divide the prawn noodles between four warm bowls and serve immediately, with lime wedges.

teriyaki swordfish with spinach and coconut

This tasty dish presents a real infusion of flavours. A teriyaki marinade adds an oriental flavour to firm, meaty swordfish, while the accompanying coconut gravy – based on reduced-fat coconut milk – is full of aromatic spices. The griddled swordfish is served on a bed of leafy spinach, a good source of iron, calcium and vitamins A and C.

SERVES 4

4 swordfish steaks, each about 150g (5oz)
2 teaspoons olive oil
4 tablespoons teriyaki sauce
1 garlic clove, peeled and crushed
2 tablespoons Madras curry paste
1 tablespoon tomato purée
400ml can reduced-fat coconut milk
squeeze of lemon juice
350g (12oz) baby leaf spinach
freshly ground black pepper

1 Place the swordfish steaks in a non-metallic dish and season with pepper. Mix together the olive oil, teriyaki sauce and garlic, then drizzle over the swordfish. Set aside for 5 minutes.

2 Heat a medium saucepan, add the curry paste and tomato purée and fry for 30 seconds. Pour in the coconut milk and simmer for 5 minutes. Finish with a squeeze of lemon juice to taste.

3 Heat a non-stick griddle pan until very hot. Add the swordfish steaks and griddle for 2–3 minutes on each side. Pour in the teriyaki marinade and allow to bubble, spooning it over the swordfish steaks to glaze.

4 In the meantime, put the spinach in a large pan (with just the water clinging to the leaves after washing), cover and cook for 30 seconds or until just wilted. Stir and season with a little pepper.

5 Place the wilted spinach in the centre of each serving plate, top with the swordfish steaks and drizzle over the coconut gravy.

smoked haddock tortilla

This Spanish-style omelette, flavoured with smoked haddock and onions, is easy to make and packed full of protein. Buy naturally smoked haddock in preference to the artificially coloured type. Cooking the onions slowly brings out their natural sweetness, which complements the spicy broad bean and tomato salsa.

SERVES 4–6

*450g (1lb) medium waxy potatoes, peeled
   and halved*
*225g (8oz) skinless, naturally smoked
   haddock fillet*
2 teaspoons olive oil
2 Spanish onions, peeled and finely sliced
6 eggs
freshly ground black pepper
FOR THE SALSA:
*300g (11oz) baby broad beans, cooked
   and skinned*
3 plum tomatoes, chopped
1 tablespoon tomato ketchup
good dash of Tabasco sauce

1   Par-boil the potatoes in water for about 8–10 minutes until only just tender, then drain. When cool enough to handle, thickly slice the potatoes. Cut the smoked haddock into thin slivers and set aside.

2   Heat the olive oil in a large non-stick frying pan (suitable for use under the grill). Add the onions, cover and steam-fry for 5 minutes, stirring occasionally. Remove the lid and cook for 8 minutes or until the onions are soft and golden. Stir in the sliced potatoes and cook for a further 2 minutes.

3   Preheat the grill. Beat the eggs in a bowl and season with pepper. Pour the beaten egg into the frying pan and scatter the smoked haddock slivers on top. Cook the tortilla, gently shaking the pan, for 4 minutes or until it is just set underneath.

4   Place the pan under the grill and cook the tortilla for a further 3 minutes or until golden and just set on top. Meanwhile, mix the salsa ingredients together in a bowl and season with pepper to taste.

5   Turn out the tortilla on to a warm serving plate and cut into wedges. Serve immediately, with the tomato and broad bean salsa.

seared tuna with green beans and basil

Fresh tuna is rich in valuable omega-3 fish oils. These oils are beneficial because they help to maintain a healthy heart. Blanching the French beans for just a few minutes in boiling water before plunging them into cold water helps to retain their colour and nutrients.

SERVES 4

1 teaspoon olive oil
4 fresh tuna steaks, each about 150g (5oz)
2 tablespoons balsamic vinegar
450g (1lb) baby new potatoes
225g (8oz) French beans, trimmed
200g (7oz) cherry tomatoes, halved
1/2 bunch of spring onions, trimmed and
  finely chopped
freshly ground black pepper
FOR THE PISTOU:
2 garlic cloves, peeled
large bunch of basil
2 tablespoons extra virgin olive oil
juice of 1/2 orange

1 Sprinkle the olive oil over the tuna steaks and rub in with your fingertips. Place in a non-metallic dish, grind over pepper and drizzle over the balsamic vinegar. Set aside for 15 minutes.

2 Boil the potatoes until tender, then drain and set aside to cool. Add the French beans to a pan of boiling water and blanch for 2–3 minutes, then drain and refresh in cold water. Drain thoroughly and tip into a bowl. Add the potatoes, tomatoes and spring onions, and toss to mix.

3 To make the pistou, put the garlic, basil, olive oil and orange juice into a small food processor and process until blended. Season to taste.

4 Heat a non-stick griddle pan until it is really hot. Add the tuna steaks and sear for about 2 minutes on each side until cooked.

5 Pour two-thirds of the pistou over the salad and gently mix together. Arrange the salad on four serving plates, top each with a seared tuna steak and spoon over the remaining pistou. Serve at once.

pan-fried smoked salmon salad with avocado

For a different way of serving smoked salmon, try it quickly flashed in the pan and served with salad, avocado and a warm tomato and chive dressing. Avocado is rich in vitamin E, a good source of potassium and high in monosaturated fatty acids.

SERVES 4

2 plum tomatoes
3 tablespoons olive oil
bunch of chives, roughly chopped
juice of 1/2 lemon
225g (8oz) smoked salmon slices
120g bag of mixed salad leaves
1 large, ripe avocado, halved, stoned, peeled
  and sliced
freshly ground black pepper

1   Immerse the plum tomatoes in a bowl of boiling hot water for 30 seconds or so, then remove and peel away the skin. Halve, deseed and thinly slice the tomatoes.

2   Heat 2 1/2 tablespoons olive oil in a small pan. Add the plum tomatoes, chives and a good squeeze of lemon juice. Season to taste and gently heat through.

3   Heat the remaining olive oil in a non-stick frying pan. Add the salmon pieces, grind over a little black pepper and cook for 30 seconds on each side.

4   Divide the salad leaves between four serving plates and top with the avocado slices. Arrange the smoked salmon slices, slightly folded, on the avocado. Spoon over the hot tomato and chive dressing and serve at once.

oily fish

Oily fish is a great source of protein and rich in the beneficial omega-3 oils. It is tasty, readily available and moderately priced, and we should all aim to eat some at least once or twice a week.

Buy fresh oily fish on the day you are going to eat it. Check that whole fish have clear eyes and gleaming scales or skin, or for convenience, buy fillets or steaks from the fish counter. However you cook your fish, don't overdo it, or it will become dry.

Of course, you don't have to buy fresh to enjoy oily fish, because it is the original convenience food. Simply reach to your cupboard for a nutritious can of salmon, mackerel, anchovies or sardines. These fabulous little cans can transform into the quickest of suppers – squashed on to bread, popped into a steaming jacket potato and even blitzed with low-fat cream cheese for an instant pâté to serve with crusty bread. Each of the following recipes serves 4.

▲ salmon sushi

Thinly slice 400g (14oz) skinless salmon fillet crossways; lay in a dish. Mix 2 tbsp extra virgin olive oil, juice of 1 lemon and ½ lime, 1 diced deseeded red chilli, 4 finely sliced spring onions and pepper; scatter on the salmon and marinate for 20 minutes. Cook 225g (8oz) Thai fragrant rice, cool slightly and toss with juice of ½ lime and pepper. Pack into cups, unmould on to plates and top with coriander. Surround with the salmon and thin avocado slices. Spoon the marinade over to serve.

anchovy and tuna jackets

Rub 4 scrubbed baking potatoes all over with 1 tsp olive oil and bake at 200°C, gas 6 for about 1 hour until tender. Toss 2 drained 160g cans yellow fin tuna in spring water with a rinsed 400g can cannellini beans, 50g can anchovy fillets, finely chopped, plus oil, 1 finely sliced red onion, the grated zest and juice of 1 lemon, 4 tbsp chopped parsley, and pepper. Split the baked potatoes, fill with the tuna salad and serve.

baked oaty mackerel fillets

Lay 8 mackerel fillets, flesh-side up, on a non-stick baking sheet. Spread with 4 tbsp wholegrain mustard and coat with 10 crushed oat cakes. Bake at 200°C, gas 6 for 10 minutes. Meanwhile, cook 4 peeled, chopped large Cox's apples in a non-stick pan with the grated zest and juice of ½ lemon for 5–6 minutes until tender but holding their shape. Stir in 2 tsp thyme leaves and pepper to taste. Serve the mackerel with the apple sauce and green beans or mangetout.

▲ lemon and sardine chunky fish pittas

Mix 100g (3½oz) cream cheese with the finely grated zest of 1 lemon and pepper to taste. Gently stir in 2 x 120g cans sardines in tomato sauce, keeping the mixture chunky. Brush 4 wholemeal pitta breads with a little olive oil and cook on a hot non-stick griddle pan for 1 minute each side until charred and crispy. Split the pitta breads and divide the sardine mixture between them. Top each with a handful of rocket leaves and serve with lemon wedges.

seared trout with sweet potato wedges

Trout is another oily fish that is high in protein and contains those helpful omega-3 oils. I cut the sweet potatoes into chunky pieces, so they don't absorb too much oil, and leave the skins on, to keep the wedges in shape and provide added fibre. You can use regular potatoes if you prefer – they'll just take a little longer to cook. A piquant citrus and caper dressing cuts through the richness of the trout beautifully.

SERVES 4

3 medium sweet potatoes, scrubbed

2 tablespoons Worcestershire sauce

3 tablespoons olive oil

2 large rainbow trout, filleted

juice of 1 large orange

juice of ½ lemon

2 tablespoons small capers, drained

1 tablespoon chopped parsley

freshly ground black pepper

1 Preheat the oven to 200°C (fan oven 180°C), gas mark 6. Cut the sweet potatoes into thick wedges and place in a large bowl. Add the Worcestershire sauce and 2 tablespoons olive oil and toss to mix. Transfer to a large roasting tray and season with pepper. Bake for 30–35 minutes until golden and crisp.

2 Meanwhile, heat a non-stick griddle pan until very hot. Brush the flesh side of the trout fillets with the remaining olive oil and season well with pepper. Place the fillets, flesh-side down, in the pan and cook for 2 minutes on each side. Remove from the pan and arrange on serving plates.

3 Add the orange and lemon juices, capers and parsley to the pan and allow to bubble for a few seconds. Spoon the warm dressing over the trout fillets and serve, with the roasted sweet potato wedges.

chilli salmon with courgette and lemon pilaf

Just a touch of chilli really brings out all the fresh flavours in this dish, which is packed with protein and vitamins. As lemon is added to the pilaf unpeeled, it should be an unwaxed lemon. If you cannot obtain one, simply scrub your lemon well in hot water before use.

SERVES 4

225g (8oz) basmati rice
2 teaspoons olive oil
1 onion, peeled and finely chopped
2 garlic cloves, peeled and crushed
4 courgettes, chopped
1 small unwaxed lemon, cut into quarters

600ml (1 pint) vegetable stock
4 boneless, skinless salmon fillets, each about
  150g (5oz)
4 teaspoons sweet chilli dipping sauce
3 tablespoons chopped coriander leaves
freshly ground black pepper

1   Rinse the basmati rice in a sieve under cold running water and set aside to drain.

2   Heat the olive oil in a large shallow pan. Add the onion and garlic and cook gently for 5 minutes or until softened. Stir in the rice, courgettes and lemon quarters, and cook for 1 minute.

3   Pour in the stock and bring to the boil. Cover and cook over a low heat for 15 minutes until all the stock has been absorbed and the rice is tender.

4   Meanwhile, preheat the grill. Lay the salmon on a non-stick baking sheet, grind over black pepper and spread each fillet with a teaspoon of chilli sauce. Grill for 5–6 minutes or until cooked through and lightly charred.

5   Season the pilaf to taste and stir in the chopped coriander. Spoon on to four serving plates, discarding the lemon if you prefer, and place the salmon fillets alongside.

roasted salmon on black toasts

Steam, griddle or oven bake, rather than deep-fry fish, to create flavourful dishes using the minimum of fat. Here baked salmon strips are served on tangy olive tapenade toasts – a healthy alternative to a hollandaise or creamy sauce. Top with a zesty, peppery salad that provides iron and vitamin C for a healthy lunch or supper.

SERVES 4

575g (1¼lb) thick salmon fillet
juice of ½ lemon
1 tablespoon olive oil
4 thick slices of ciabatta bread
4 tablespoons black olive tapenade
freshly ground black pepper
FOR THE SALAD:
75g (3oz) watercress, trimmed
1 red onion, peeled and thinly sliced
2 large oranges, segmented

1 Preheat the oven to 200°C (fan oven 180°C), gas mark 6. Cut the salmon into 8 equal strips and lay these on a non-stick baking tray. Drizzle over the lemon juice and half the olive oil, and season with pepper. Bake for 8–10 minutes or until the salmon is just cooked.

2 For the salad, toss the watercress sprigs, onion slices and orange segments together in a bowl. Season with a little pepper.

3 Meanwhile, heat a large non-stick griddle pan and brush with the remaining olive oil. Griddle the ciabatta slices for 2 minutes on each side or until golden and crisp. Spread the ciabatta toasts with the olive tapenade and place on four serving plates. Lay two strips of salmon on each toast. Top with the watercress salad and serve.

spiced griddled mackerel with spinach lentils

The spinach lentils in this healthy dish can easily be made ahead if required and reheated. Lentils are extremely nutritious, being a good source of protein, fibre, vitamin B, calcium, iron and phosphorus. Here they are served with spiced mackerel – a fine fish that's rich in beneficial omega-3 oils.

SERVES 4
2 tablespoons coriander seeds
1 tablespoon coarsely ground black pepper
4 tablespoons roughly chopped flat leaf parsley
8 small mackerel fillets
1 tablespoon olive oil
FOR THE SPINACH LENTILS:
1 tablespoon sunflower oil
1 large onion, peeled and chopped
4 garlic cloves, peeled and crushed
1 tablespoon garam masala
350g (12oz) split red lentils, rinsed
1.2 litres (2 pints) vegetable stock
225g (8oz) spinach leaves, roughly chopped

1   To release the flavour from the coriander seeds, pound with a pestle and mortar, or place them in a polythene bag and crush with a rolling pin. Tip into a bowl and mix with the pepper and parsley.

2   Rub the flesh side of the mackerel fillets with the olive oil, then sprinkle with the spice mix and press to adhere. Set to one side.

3   For the spinach lentils, heat the sunflower oil in a large pan. Add the onion and steam-fry for 5 minutes. Add the garlic and garam masala and cook for a further minute. Stir in the lentils and stock, bring to the boil and simmer for 15–20 minutes or until the lentils are just tender.

4   Heat a non-stick griddle pan over a medium heat. When hot, add the mackerel fillets, skin-side down, and cook for 2–3 minutes. Turn carefully and cook for a further 2 minutes.

5   Stir the spinach into the lentils and cook briefly until just wilted. Spoon on to four serving plates and top each serving with two mackerel fillets.

4 chicken and turkey

citrus roasted chicken with tzatziki

This is one of my favourite ways of cooking chicken. Removing the backbone and flattening the bird helps it to cook more quickly and evenly, keeping the breast meat moist. I like to serve this citrus roast with a homemade tzatziki but if time is short, you can buy a tub of ready-made.

SERVES 4

1 free-range or organic chicken, about
  1.6kg (3½lb)
handful of thyme sprigs
1 large orange, cut into quarters
2 unwaxed lemons, halved
freshly ground black pepper

FOR THE TZATZIKI:
½ cucumber
200g (7oz) Greek yogurt
1 garlic clove, peeled and crushed
1 tablespoon extra virgin olive oil
20g (¾oz) mint leaves, chopped
lemon juice, to taste

1   Preheat the oven to 200°C (fan oven 180°C), gas mark 6. Lay the chicken, breast-side down, on a board. Using poultry shears or a sharp pair of scissors, cut down either side of the backbone. Turn the chicken over and press to flatten, using the heel of your hand. Season generously with pepper and place, breast-side down, in a roasting tin or tray. Scatter the thyme over and roast for 30 minutes.

2   Remove the roasting tin from the oven and reduce the setting to 180°C (fan oven 160°C), gas mark 4. Squeeze the juice from the orange and lemons over the chicken, then add the spent citrus peel pieces to the tray and turn the chicken over. Roast for a further 30–40 minutes until the chicken is cooked through. To test, pierce the thickest part of the thigh with a skewer: the juices should run clear: if they are pink, return to the oven for a little longer.

3   Meanwhile, make the tzatziki. Coarsely grate the cucumber, squeeze out the excess liquid, then place in a bowl. Add the yogurt, garlic, olive oil, mint and lemon juice, and black pepper to taste.

4   Remove the chicken from the oven, cover with foil and leave to rest in a warm place for 10 minutes before serving. Serve the chicken with the tzatziki, and a watercress salad if you like.

polenta crusted chicken

These crispy baked chicken thighs, coated in Cajun spiced polenta, are equally delicious hot or cold. Polenta is a good source of carbohydrate and gluten-free, so it's especially useful for anyone with an intolerance to this wheat-based protein.

SERVES 4

8 skinless chicken thigh fillets
juice of 1 lime
2 tablespoons Cajun spice
4 tablespoons polenta
½ tablespoon olive oil
1 large onion, peeled and sliced

3 red peppers, cored, deseeded and sliced
pinch of sugar
1 large garlic clove, peeled and crushed
150ml (¼ pint) vegetable stock
150ml (¼ pint) tomato juice
freshly ground black pepper
watercress sprigs, to serve

1 Preheat the oven to 200°C (fan oven 180°C), gas mark 6. Open out the chicken thighs and squeeze the lime juice over. Sprinkle with half of the Cajun spice and re-roll.

2 Toss the polenta with the remaining Cajun spice and spread out on a plate. Turn the rolled chicken thighs in the polenta to coat evenly, pressing with your fingertips to ensure the coating adheres. Transfer the chicken to a roasting tin and bake for 35–40 minutes until golden and cooked through.

3 Meanwhile, heat the olive oil in a large pan. Add the onion and red peppers, cover with a damp piece of greaseproof paper and put the lid on the pan. Cook gently for 15 minutes until very soft. Stir in the sugar, garlic, stock and tomato juice. Cover again and cook for a further 10 minutes. Cool slightly, then whiz in a blender or food processor until smooth. Season with pepper to taste.

4 Serve the polenta crusted chicken with the red pepper gravy and watercress sprigs. Roasted new potatoes (see page 86) make an excellent accompaniment.

apple roast chicken and new potatoes

Roasting chicken on the bone keeps it moist and tasty. To crisp the skin and lose as much fat as possible, the chicken pieces are first roasted on a rack, then on a bed of apples flavoured with rosemary and cider. Apples provide vitamin C and fibre.

Illustrated on previous page

SERVES 4

4 free-range or organic chicken thighs
4 free-range or organic chicken drumsticks
juice of 1/2 lemon
1 tablespoon olive oil
2 red onions, peeled, halved and each half cut
  into 4 chunks
200ml (7fl oz) dry cider
150ml (1/4 pint) chicken stock
3 medium Cox's apples, cored and cut into
  6 wedges
3 rosemary sprigs
FOR THE ROASTED NEW POTATOES:
675g (1 1/2 lb) Charlotte potatoes, halved
  lengthways
2 teaspoons olive oil

1   Preheat the oven to 200°C (fan oven 180°C), gas mark 6. For the roasted potatoes, place the potatoes in a roasting tray and drizzle with the 2 teaspoons olive oil. Roast in the top of the oven for 35–40 minutes until tender and crisp.

2   Place the chicken on a rack over a roasting tin and squeeze over the lemon juice. Roast, skin-side up, on a shelf below the potatoes for 20–25 minutes.

3   Meanwhile, heat the olive oil in a pan and steam-fry the onions over a medium heat for 10–15 minutes until beginning to soften and brown. Uncover and pour in the cider and stock. Bring to the boil and simmer gently for 5 minutes.

4   Transfer the chicken pieces to a plate. Remove any fat from the roasting tin, then add the onion and cider mixture. Add the apples and rosemary, then sit the chicken pieces, skin-side up, on top. Roast for a further 15–20 minutes until the chicken is cooked through. Serve with the roasted potatoes.

maple roasted poussins

Poussins are now widely available and inexpensive, and make a change from chicken. Here they are flavoured simply with rosemary and garlic, and glazed with maple syrup – to delicious effect. I like to serve them with hot new potatoes and a crisp endive and walnut salad.

SERVES 4

4 poussins
4 rosemary sprigs
4 garlic cloves, peeled and lightly crushed
2 tablespoons maple syrup
1 tablespoon Dijon mustard
2 teaspoons olive oil
freshly ground black pepper

1 Preheat the oven to 200°C (fan oven 180°C), gas mark 6. Stuff the poussin cavities with the rosemary and garlic, then loosely tie up the legs with kitchen string.

2 In a small bowl, mix together the maple syrup, mustard, olive oil and some black pepper. Place the poussins in a roasting tray and pour over the maple syrup glaze.

3 Roast in the oven for 40–45 minutes, basting occasionally, until golden and cooked through. Serve with hot new potatoes and a crisp salad, or green vegetable.

steamed tarragon chicken

Gently steaming chicken breasts with leeks and aromatic tarragon in one pot is a healthy way of cooking and keeps the meat moist and full of taste. A creamy, low-fat mustard and tarragon sauce is the perfect partner. All you need is a simple accompaniment, such as baked potatoes.

SERVES 4

4 skinless chicken breast fillets, each about
*   150g (5 oz)*
4 leeks, trimmed
1 tablespoon olive oil
150ml (¼ pint) white wine
8 tarragon sprigs
freshly ground black pepper

FOR THE SAUCE:

5 tablespoons half-fat crème fraîche
1 garlic clove, peeled and crushed
2 teaspoons Dijon mustard
2 tablespoons chopped tarragon

1   Cut each of the chicken breasts lengthways into 4 pieces. Slice the leeks into 2cm (¾ inch) pieces. Heat the olive oil in a large sauté pan, add the leeks and gently steam-fry for 10 minutes. Add the wine and boil rapidly until it has almost totally reduced.

2   Scatter the tarragon sprigs over the leeks and lay the chicken pieces on top. Season with black pepper. Cover with a damp piece of greaseproof paper and put the lid on the pan. Cook very gently for 15–18 minutes until the chicken is cooked.

3   Meanwhile, to make the sauce, combine the crème fraîche, garlic, mustard and chopped tarragon in a bowl and stir until evenly blended. Season with pepper to taste.

4   Serve the steamed chicken and leeks with a generous spoonful of the creamy tarragon sauce.

sun blushed chicken pockets

Chicken breasts are filled with sun-blushed tomatoes and low-fat cream cheese, then wrapped in Italian pancetta and baked. A healthy stir-fry of Italian style greens flavoured with garlic, a hint of olive oil and a squeeze of lemon is the perfect complement.

SERVES 4

4 skinless chicken breast fillets, each about
150g (5oz)
4 tablespoons low-fat cream cheese
12 sun-blushed tomatoes, roughly chopped
4 slices of pancetta
freshly ground black pepper

FOR THE GREENS:
1 tablespoon olive oil
2 garlic cloves, peeled and crushed
300g (11oz) cavolo nero, spring greens or
green cabbage, cored and finely shredded
squeeze of lemon juice

1 Preheat the oven to 200°C (fan oven 180°C), gas mark 6. Remove the small fillet from the underside of each chicken breast and set aside. Make a vertical cut down the length of each chicken breast, but not all the way through, to form a pocket.

2 Mix the cream cheese with the tomatoes and season with pepper. Put a spoonful into each chicken breast pocket. Fold over the flaps of the pocket and cover with the reserved fillets to enclose the filling.

3 Loosely wrap a slice of pancetta around each chicken breast. Heat a large non-stick frying pan (preferably ovenproof), add the chicken and sear for 2 minutes on each side until golden. Transfer to the oven and bake for 12–15 minutes or until the chicken is cooked through. (If your pan isn't ovenproof, transfer the chicken to a roasting tray.)

4 Just before serving, heat the olive oil in a non stick wok, add the garlic and fry gently for 30 seconds. Add the shredded cabbage and stir-fry for 3–4 minutes until wilted, but still retaining a bite. Add a squeeze of lemon juice and pepper to taste. Serve the chicken parcels on the stir-fried cabbage.

tapenade chicken with lemon Puy lentils

Tapenade, or black olive paste, is one of the jewels in my storecupboard. It makes a tasty stuffing for chicken, and you can vary the flavour by substituting green olive or red pepper tapenade. I wrap these stuffed chicken breasts in Parma ham and serve them on lemony Puy lentils – another storecupboard favourite. These quick cooking lentils don't need to be pre-soaked and they're a good source of B vitamins, iron and fibre.

SERVES 4

4 skinless chicken breast fillets, each about
   150g (5oz)
4 tablespoons black olive tapenade
4 slices of Parma ham
4 bay leaves
1 teaspoon olive oil
freshly ground black pepper

FOR THE LEMON PUY LENTILS:
300g (11oz) Puy lentils
1 litre (1³/₄ pints) chicken or vegetable stock
4 tablespoons extra virgin olive oil
grated zest and juice of 1 lemon
225g (8oz) baby or young leaf spinach

1   Preheat the oven to 200°C (fan oven 180°C), gas mark 6. For the lemon Puy lentils, put the lentils in a pan with the stock. Bring to the boil and simmer for 20–25 minutes until the lentils are tender.

2   Meanwhile, place the chicken breasts on a board and remove the small fillet from the underside of each breast; set aside. Make a vertical cut down the length of the chicken breast, but not all the way through, to create a pocket. Season all over with pepper.

3   Place a tablespoon of olive tapenade in the pocket of each chicken breast. Fold over the flaps of the pocket and cover with the reserved fillets to enclose the filling. Wrap a piece of Parma ham around each chicken breast and tuck in a bay leaf. Brush lightly with the olive oil.

4   Heat a large non-stick frying pan (preferably ovenproof), add the chicken and sear for 2 minutes on each side until golden. Transfer to the oven and bake for 12–15 minutes or until the chicken is cooked through. (If your pan isn't ovenproof, transfer the chicken to a roasting tray.)

5   When cooked, drain the lentils and return to the pan. Stir in the olive oil, lemon zest and juice. Return to the heat and gently warm through, then add the spinach and stir until wilted. Season with pepper to taste. Serve the chicken with the Puy lentils.

chicken and prune ragout

I am a huge fan of ready-to-eat juicy prunes, keeping a supply in my cupboard for healthy instant snacking. Prunes are rich in fibre and antioxidants, and they go well in savoury dishes. Don't be put off by the number of garlic cloves in this recipe – they mellow and sweeten as they roast in their skins. Serve this ragout with cous cous, rice or fluffy mashed potato.

SERVES 4

3 large red onions, peeled and each cut into
  8 wedges
2 tablespoons olive oil
8 whole garlic cloves (unpeeled)
4 skinless chicken breast fillets, each about
  150g (5oz)
200ml (7 fl oz) red wine
250g (9oz) prunes
4 thyme sprigs
150ml (¼ pint) hot chicken stock

1 Preheat the oven to 200°C (fan oven 180°C), gas mark 6. Put the onion wedges in a roasting tin and drizzle 1 tablespoon olive oil over them. Roast for 20 minutes, then add the garlic cloves and roast for a further 10 minutes.

2 Meanwhile, using a small knife, slash the top of each chicken breast in a criss-cross fashion, taking care not to cut all the way through. Put the chicken in a shallow dish and pour over the remaining olive oil and 50ml (2fl oz) of the red wine. Leave to marinate for 20 minutes.

3 Heat a large non-stick frying pan over a medium-high heat. Remove the chicken from the marinade, add to the frying pan and sear for 2 minutes on each side or until golden brown.

4 Scatter the prunes and thyme over the roasted onions and garlic, then pour over the remaining wine and the stock. Place the seared chicken breasts on top and bake in the oven for 15–20 minutes or until the chicken is cooked through.

chicken korma

My light version of this popular rich Indian curry is delicious and creamy but much lower in fat than anything you might order as a takeaway. I use half-fat coconut milk, natural yogurt and almonds to enrich the curry. If you want more heat, add chilli flakes with the spices. Serve with the refreshing relish, and basmati rice or chapattis.

SERVES 4

2 tablespoons sunflower oil
2 large onions, peeled and finely sliced
12 skinless chicken thigh fillets, halved
3 garlic cloves, peeled and crushed
1 tablespoon garam masala
2 teaspoons ground turmeric
1 bay leaf
450ml (³/4 pint) chicken stock
150ml (¹/4 pint) low-fat coconut milk

75ml (2¹/2 fl oz) natural yogurt
2 tablespoons ground almonds
20g (³/4oz) mint leaves, chopped

FOR THE RELISH:
4 ripe tomatoes, chopped
1 small red onion, peeled and finely chopped
20g (³/4oz) coriander leaves, roughly chopped
squeeze of lemon juice
freshly ground black pepper

1   Heat 1 tablespoon oil in a large, shallow pan. Add the onions and steam-fry for 10 minutes until softened. Uncover and fry for a further 5 minutes until beginning to brown.

2   Meanwhile, heat the remaining sunflower oil in a large non-stick frying pan, add the chicken pieces and sauté for about 2 minutes on each side or until golden.

3   Add the garlic and spices to the onions and fry, stirring, for about 1 minute, then add the sautéed chicken pieces and bay leaf. Pour in the stock and bring to the boil. Simmer gently for 15–20 minutes or until the chicken is cooked

4   In the meantime, prepare the relish. Combine the tomatoes, red onion and coriander in a bowl. Toss to mix and add lemon juice and black pepper to taste. Set aside.

5   Stir the coconut milk, yogurt, almonds and mint into the korma. Warm through, but do not boil or the coconut milk will separate. Season to taste and serve straightaway.

chicken and sesame stir-fry with noodles

This stir-fry is fast, colourful and packed with nutrients. Broccoli is an important source of vitamins and minerals, including antioxidants that may help to reduce the risk of heart disease and some forms of cancer. Stir-frying helps to preserve the vitamin C content.

SERVES 4

2 large skinless chicken breast fillets
1 tablespoon olive oil
1 garlic clove, peeled and crushed
5cm (2 inch) piece fresh root ginger, peeled and
   finely chopped
225g (8oz) broccoli florets
2 large carrots

1 bunch of spring onions, trimmed
250g (9oz) medium egg noodles
2 tablespoons soy sauce
1 tablespoon thin honey
juice of 1 orange
1 tablespoon sesame seeds, toasted
freshly ground black pepper

1 Cut the chicken breasts into thin strips and place in a bowl with the olive oil, garlic and ginger. Toss to mix and set to one side.

2 Put the broccoli florets in a heatproof bowl, cover with boiling water and leave to stand for 1 minute. Drain, refresh under cold running water and drain well. Cut the carrots into thin matchstick strips. Halve the spring onions and cut into strips lengthways.

3 Heat a large non-stick wok or non-stick pan, add the chicken and stir-fry for 2 minutes. Add the carrots, broccoli and 1 tablespoon water. Cover with a lid and steam-fry for 4–5 minutes until the chicken is cooked, adding the spring onions for the last minute.

4 Meanwhile, cook the noodles according to the packet instructions. In a bowl, mix together the soy sauce, honey and orange juice.

5 Drain the noodles thoroughly and add to the pan with the soy mixture. Toss well until everything is piping hot. Season and scatter over the sesame seeds. Serve at once, in warm bowls.

roast chicken and leftovers

A golden bird roasted with the merest drizzle of olive oil, a squeeze of lemon and some pepper is an unbeatable Sunday lunch. Organic or free-range chickens will give a much better flavour than factory farmed birds. Simply roast at 200°C (fan oven 180°C), gas mark 6 for 20 minutes per 500g (1lb) plus an extra 20 minutes, until the juices run clear. Roast breast-side down for half the cooking time, breast-side up for the remainder. And, for a healthy approach, serve with a fresh fruit salsa or garlicky raita rather than a gravy that's high in fat.

Oven-steaming is an excellent option for chicken or turkey breast. Loosely wrap in foil with a splash of wine, a slice of lemon or some fresh herbs, then place in the oven at the same temperature until cooked through, 20–25 minutes for chicken (longer for turkey). Invariably you'll have meat left over from a roast for a nourishing soup or the following tasty recipes; each serves 4.

▲ chicken and avocado on rye
Mix the chopped flesh of 1 large, ripe avocado with a squeeze of lime juice, 1 finely chopped shallot, 1 small crushed garlic clove, a dash of Tabasco, 2 tbsp Greek yogurt and 4 quartered cherry tomatoes; season. Top 4 slices of rye bread with 50g (2oz) cooked, sliced chicken breast or turkey. Spoon the guacamole on top and finish with a spoonful of rich tomato chutney. Serve each open sandwich with a lime wedge.

chicken and artichoke pain bagnes

Cut each of 4 wholemeal baps into 3 slices horizontally, toast on both sides, then rub with a cut garlic clove. Thinly slice 225g (8oz) cooked chicken breast and 3 plum tomatoes; quarter 4 roasted artichokes in oil. Layer half these ingredients on the base of the baps. Season with pepper and torn basil. Press on the middle toasted bap slices and repeat the filling layer. Position the bap tops and press down gently to serve.

spicy hot chicken and prune baguettes

Mix 6 tbsp light mayonnaise with 6 tbsp Greek yogurt and 2 heaped tsp Thai red curry paste in a bowl. Add 125g (4oz) chopped, ready-to eat-prunes and 125g (4oz) cooked chicken, torn into strips. Mix well; season. In another bowl, toss ½ finely sliced red onion with 4 handfuls of rocket leaves and a good squeeze of lime juice; season. Split 4 submarine rolls and toast, cut-side down, on a hot non-stick griddle pan. Sandwich together with the chicken mixture and rocket salad to serve.

▲ Mediterranean-style bread salad

Toast 3 split white pitta breads on both sides until crisp. Combine 175g (6oz) torn, cooked chicken, 1 chopped deseeded cucumber, 6 quartered small vine tomatoes, 1 thinly sliced red onion, 20 pitted black olives and 20g (¾oz) roughly chopped flat leaf parsley in a bowl. Whisk 2 tbsp extra virgin olive oil with 3 crushed garlic cloves, juice of 1 lemon and pepper; use to dress the salad. Break the crispy pittas over the salad and toss gently stir to serve.

hot sesame chicken and avocado salad

Packed with flavour, this tasty, quick and easy dish includes my favourite fruit, the avocado. Regarded as a 'super food', avocado contains more protein than any other fruit, plenty of vitamin E and useful potassium. It is also rich in monounsaturated fatty acids, which provide energy and are believed to help maintain a healthy heart. Serve this light, healthy lunch or supper with crusty, warm Granary bread to mop up the delicious juices.

SERVES 4

2 large skinless chicken breast fillets
3 tablespoons wholegrain mustard
1 tablespoon thin honey
juice of 1 lemon
1/2 tablespoon sunflower oil

1 ripe avocado, stoned, peeled and sliced
large handful of crisp salad leaves, such as
   Little Gem lettuce
2 tablespoons sesame seeds
1 teaspoon sesame oil
freshly ground black pepper

1 Cut the chicken breasts into finger-sized strips and place in a bowl. Season with black pepper and add the mustard, honey and lemon juice. Toss the chicken to mix well.

2 Heat the sunflower oil in a non-stick wok or large non-stick frying pan until very hot. Add the chicken mixture and stir-fry for 5–6 minutes or until golden and cooked. Meanwhile, toss the avocado slices with the salad leaves and pile on to four large plates.

3 Add the sesame seeds to the chicken and cook for a further minute or until the seeds are just beginning to colour. Spoon the hot sesame chicken on top of the salad leaves, drizzle with the sesame oil and serve at once.

Thai green turkey burgers

These low fat, high protein turkey burgers contain naturally sweet grated carrot to keep them moist. Flavoured with Thai green curry paste and spring onions, the burgers are served in ciabatta rolls with salad leaves and mango chutney.

SERVES 4

450g (1lb) lean turkey mince
125g (4oz) grated carrot (3 medium carrots)
4 spring onions, trimmed and chopped
1¹/₂ tablespoons Thai green curry paste
1 small egg white
1 tablespoon groundnut oil

TO SERVE:
4 ciabatta rolls
handful of crisp salad leaves, such as rocket
4 cherry tomatoes, sliced
mango chutney, to taste

1   In a large bowl, mix the minced turkey with the grated carrot, spring onions and Thai green curry paste. Add the egg white and stir well to combine.

2   Divide the turkey mixture into four equal portions and shape into burgers. Place on a small board or flat plate, cover with cling film and chill in the refrigerator for 20 minutes.

3   Heat the groundnut oil in a large non-stick frying pan. Add the turkey burgers and cook for 5–7 minutes on each side or until golden and cooked through.

4   Split the ciabatta rolls. Serve the burgers in the rolls with crisp salad leaves, cherry tomato slices and a good spoonful of mango chutney.

turkey steaks with zesty gremolata

These turkey steaks are simply griddled and finished with an unusual topping of crispy ciabatta crumbs flavoured with parsley, lemon and garlic. Sweet roasted green beans and tomatoes make a delicious accompaniment. Tomatoes are particularly good for you as they contain vitamins C and E, potassium and carotenoids, including lycopene, which is an antioxidant that may help to reduce the risk of certain forms of cancer.

SERVES 4

4 turkey steaks, each about 125g (4oz)
grated zest and juice of 1 lemon
1 tablespoon olive oil
1 ready-to-bake ciabatta roll, coarsely grated
1 garlic clove, peeled and finely chopped
20g (3/4oz) flat leaf parsley, chopped
freshly ground black pepper
FOR THE ROASTED BEANS AND TOMATOES:
250g (9oz) baby plum tomatoes
250g (9oz) fine green beans, trimmed
1 tablespoon olive oil

1   Preheat the oven to 200°C (fan oven 180°C), gas mark 6. Place each turkey steak between two pieces of cling film or greaseproof paper and beat to a 5mm (1/4 inch) thickness, using a rolling pin. Lay the turkey steaks in a shallow ovenproof dish and sprinkle with the lemon juice and olive oil. Season with pepper.

2   Place the tomatoes and green beans on a roasting tray, drizzle over the olive oil and season with pepper. Scatter the ciabatta breadcrumbs on another small roasting tray.

3   Place both roasting trays into the oven. Remove the breadcrumbs after 5 minutes; they will be crisp and golden. Continue to cook the beans and tomatoes for a further 8–10 minutes.

4   Meanwhile, heat a non-stick ridged griddle pan until very hot. Add the turkey steaks and cook for 2–3 minutes on each side. (You may have to do this in two batches.)

5   Toss the toasted crumbs, lemon zest, garlic and parsley together in a bowl and season with pepper. Place the turkey steaks on warm serving plates, spoon over the roasted beans and tomatoes, then finish with a generous scattering of gremolata crumbs. Serve at once.

aromatic turkey pilaf

Bulghar wheat, sometimes known as cracked bulghar wheat, has a good texture and a delicious nutty taste. In this pilaf it takes the place of rice. Carrots make a healthy addition as they are a rich source of beta-carotene, which is converted to vitamin A in the body. Beta-carotene may also boost the immune system and help reduce the risk of some forms of cancer. You can replace the turkey with chicken or lean pork if you like or, for a meat-free pilaf, finish with a scattering of toasted pine nuts or flaked almonds.

SERVES 4

300g (11oz) turkey breast fillet
225g (8oz) bulghar wheat, rinsed
1 tablespoon sunflower oil
1 large onion, peeled and chopped
1 garlic clove, peeled and crushed
1½ tablespoons garam masala
125g (4oz) ready-to-eat dried apricots, chopped
125g (4oz) sultanas
1 bay leaf
2 large carrots, peeled and coarsely grated
600ml–750ml (1–1¼ pints) chicken stock
4 tablespoons chopped coriander
freshly ground black pepper
1 large lemon, cut into wedges, to serve

1 Cut the turkey into 1cm (½ inch) slices and set aside. Put the bulghar wheat in a bowl and add enough cold water to cover generously. Leave to stand for 15 minutes.

2 Meanwhile, heat the sunflower oil in a large non-stick sauté pan or non-stick wok, add the onion and cook for 5 minutes until softened. Increase the heat and add the turkey. Fry, turning frequently, for 3–4 minutes or until the turkey is golden all over. Stir in the garlic and garam masala, and cook for a further minute.

3 Add the dried fruits, bay leaf and grated carrots, then pour in 600ml (1 pint) stock. Drain the bulghar wheat and add to the pan. Season with black pepper. Cover and cook gently for 15 minutes. Add extra stock if the pilaf becomes too dry; it should have the consistency of a risotto.

4 Spoon the pilaf into a large serving dish and stir in the coriander, reserving a tablespoon to scatter over the top. Serve with the lemon wedges.

5 meat

lamb steaks with minted beet and spinach salad

Lean lamb steaks are griddled and served with a salad of baby spinach, butter beans and baby beetroot in a fresh minty dressing. Butter beans provide slow release carbohydrate, and spinach is a good source of minerals and vitamins.

SERVES 4

4 lamb leg steaks, each about 140g (4¹/₂oz)

2 garlic cloves, peeled and crushed

2 tablespoons balsamic vinegar

1 tablespoon olive oil

150g (5oz) baby leaf spinach

400g can butter beans, drained and rinsed

1 red onion, peeled and thinly sliced

250g (9oz) fresh baby beetroot, cooked
   and peeled

freshly ground black pepper

mint leaves, to serve

FOR THE DRESSING:

1 tablespoon olive oil

1 tablespoon white wine vinegar

1 teaspoon Dijon mustard

pinch of sugar

4 tablespoons chopped mint

1 Place the lamb steaks in a non-metallic bowl. Add the garlic, balsamic vinegar, olive oil and plenty of black pepper. Turn the lamb steaks in the marinade to coat well, then set aside for 20 minutes, or longer in the refrigerator if possible.

2 To make the dressing, whisk the olive oil, wine vinegar, mustard, sugar and mint together in a large bowl. Season with a little black pepper. Set aside.

3 Heat a non-stick griddle pan over a medium-high heat. Add the lamb and cook for 2–3 minutes on each side for medium-rare, or longer to your liking. Pour in the marinade and allow to bubble and reduce to a glaze for the lamb steaks.

4 Meanwhile, add the spinach, butter beans and red onion to the dressing and toss gently to combine. Divide the salad between four large serving plates and top with the baby beetroot. Place the lamb steaks alongside, spoon over the pan juices and scatter with a few mint leaves to serve.

babotie burgers

There's nothing better than a real homemade burger and these spiced South African lamb burgers are particularly good. A fruity apple and mango chutney is the ideal complement.

SERVES 4 (OR 8)

4 teaspoons olive oil
1 large onion, peeled and finely chopped
1 tablespoon garam masala
1 teaspoon ground cinnamon
450g (1lb) lean lamb mince
1 large carrot, peeled and grated
50g (2oz) fresh white breadcrumbs
50g (2oz) chopped almonds

grated zest of 1 lemon
1 egg, beaten
freshly ground black pepper

FOR THE CHUTNEY:
50g (2oz) sultanas
2 Cox's apples, diced
1 tablespoon hot (spicy) mango chutney
seeds of 6 cardamom pods, crushed
2 tablespoons chopped mint

1 Preheat the oven to 180°C (fan oven 160°C), gas mark 4. Heat 2 teaspoons olive oil in a pan and gently fry the onion for 10 minutes until soft and golden. Add the garam masala and cinnamon and cook for a further minute. Tip into a large bowl and allow to cool.

2 Add the minced lamb, grated carrot, breadcrumbs, almonds and lemon zest to the cooled spiced onion and mix well. Season with pepper and add the beaten egg to bind the mixture.

3 Divide the mixture into eight portions. Roll into balls, then flatten to make small burgers. Heat the remaining olive oil in a large non-stick frying pan and sear the burgers quickly on each side.

4 Place the seared burgers on a non-stick baking tray and bake in the oven for 10–15 minutes or until cooked through. Meanwhile, mix all the ingredients for the chutney together and season to taste. Serve the burgers with the fruit chutney, crusty bread and a leafy salad.

lamb and parsnip ragout

This is real comfort food – a rich lamb stew with whole baby carrots and parsnip chunks, topped with gnocchi. It's a lighter, healthier version of a classic stew with suet dumplings. Experiment with the gnocchi by using different flavours, such as garlic and thyme, or chilli and chives, sprinkling the stew with thyme or chives to serve.

Illustrated on previous page

SERVES 4

350g (12oz) lean leg of lamb
1 tablespoon plain flour
1 tablespoon olive oil
1 onion, peeled and finely chopped
150g (5oz) baby carrots, trimmed and scrubbed
2 parsnips, peeled and cut into chunks
2 bay leaves
2 tablespoons sun-dried tomato paste
300ml (1/2 pint) red wine
450ml (3/4 pint) vegetable stock
freshly ground black pepper
2 tablespoons torn basil leaves, to sprinkle

FOR THE GARLIC GNOCCHI:

225g (8oz) plain flour
1 teaspoon baking powder
2 garlic cloves, peeled and crushed
2 tablespoons olive oil
125ml (4fl oz) milk

1 Cut the lamb into 2cm (3/4 inch) chunks and toss in the seasoned flour. Heat the olive oil in a large shallow, heavy pan and fry the lamb over a high heat until browned all over. Remove with a slotted spoon and set aside.

2 Add 2 tablespoons water and the onion to the pan. Stir well over a medium heat, scraping up the crusty golden bits from the bottom of the pan. Lower the heat, cover and steam-fry for 5 minutes, stirring occasionally.

3 Stir in the carrots, parsnips and bay leaves and cook for 2 minutes, then return the lamb to the pan. Stir in the tomato paste, red wine and stock. Bring to the boil, cover and simmer for 25–30 minutes or until the lamb and vegetables are just tender.

4 To make the gnocchi, sift the flour and baking powder into a bowl and season well. Make a well in the middle. Combine the garlic, olive oil and milk, then add to the well and gradually incorporate the flour to make a soft, but not sticky, dough.

5 Shape the dough into 16 small rounds and arrange on top of the ragout. Replace the lid and simmer for a further 10 minutes. Scatter over the basil just before serving.

steak and mushroom ciabattas with mustard sauce

Char-grilled steak strips are served in a toasted ciabatta roll with meaty mushrooms, peppery iron-rich watercress and a creamy mustard sauce, for a satisfying supper or lunch. Lean beef is a good source of easily absorbed iron and is also rich in zinc. Always allow steak to rest before cutting, as this allows the juices to be reabsorbed and keeps the meat really succulent.

SERVES 4

2 very large field mushrooms
4 teaspoons olive oil
300g (11oz) sirloin steak
1 teaspoon Worcestershire sauce
4 ready-to-bake ciabatta rolls, cooked according
  to packet instructions
85g packet watercress
freshly ground black pepper
FOR THE MUSTARD SAUCE:
2 tablespoons half-fat crème fraîche
1 tablespoon Dijon mustard
1 tablespoon wholegrain mustard

1 Preheat the grill to medium. Brush the mushrooms with 1 tablespoon olive oil and season with black pepper. Grill for 6 minutes on each side or until just cooked.

2 To make the sauce, mix the crème fraîche with the Dijon and wholegrain mustards in a small bowl until evenly blended and set aside.

3 Preheat a non-stick griddle pan until very hot. Brush the steak with the Worcestershire sauce and remaining olive oil, then season with pepper. Place on the griddle pan and sear for 2–3 minutes on each side or until cooked to your liking. Remove to a warm plate, cover loosely with foil and leave to rest for 5 minutes.

4 Cut each ciabatta roll in half and toast the cut sides under the grill for 1–2 minutes. Thinly slice the steak and mushrooms on the diagonal. Place the watercress on the bottom half of each roll and top with the steak and mushroom slices. Drizzle over the mustard sauce and cover with the lid of the roll. Serve immediately.

chilli con carne pie

You can make this chilli as hot or as cool as you like. I've used less meat than is usual, and added Puy lentils and beans. The turmeric and coriander mashed potato crust makes a tasty change from the typical chilli accompaniment of boiled rice. A little chocolate added at the end, Mexican-style, really enhances the colour and flavour.

SERVES 4–6

1 tablespoon olive oil

1 onion, peeled and finely chopped

1 garlic clove, peeled and crushed

250g (9oz) lean steak mince

2 red chillies, deseeded and finely chopped

1 teaspoon ground cumin

1 tablespoon red pepper tapenade

400g can chopped tomatoes

300ml (½ pint) vegetable stock

100g (3½oz) Puy lentils

400g can kidney beans, drained and rinsed

15g (½oz) plain dark chocolate, roughly chopped

freshly ground black pepper

FOR THE MASH:

900g (2lb) white floury potatoes, such as Maris Piper, peeled

3 tablespoons hot semi-skimmed milk

1 teaspoon ground turmeric

2 tablespoons chopped coriander

1   Heat the olive oil in a large pan, add the onion and garlic and cook for 5 minutes. Turn up the heat, add the mince and cook, stirring, for 3 minutes or until browned. Stir in the chillies and cumin and cook for 1 minute.

2   Add the tapenade, chopped tomatoes, stock, lentils and kidney beans, then bring to the boil. Simmer for 25–30 minutes. Stir in the chocolate and season with black pepper.

3   Meanwhile for the mash, cut the potatoes into even-sized chunks, add to a pan of cold water and bring to the boil. Simmer for 20 minutes or until tender, then drain. Tip the potatoes back into the pan and mash over a low heat, stirring in the milk, turmeric and coriander. Season to taste.

4   Preheat the grill. Spoon the hot chilli beef into a gratin dish and spread the hot mashed potato roughly over the top. Place under the grill for 5 minutes or until the topping is crisp and golden brown.

gingered beef curry

A really light, quick curry, cooked in a novel way. Lean, tender sirloin steak is fast griddled to remain juicy and pink, then set aside to rest. Chick peas soak up the spicy flavours of the curry sauce and shredded spring greens and the steak strips are added at the end of cooking. Serve the curry on its own, or with basmati rice or chapattis.

SERVES 4

2 sirloin steaks, each 250g (9oz)
1 tablespoon olive oil
2 onions, peeled and sliced
2 tablespoons Madras curry paste
5cm (2 inch) piece fresh root ginger, peeled
  and grated
600ml (1 pint) vegetable stock
400g can chick peas, drained and rinsed
100g (3½oz) spring greens, finely shredded
freshly coarse ground black pepper

1 Brush the steaks with a little olive oil and sprinkle with coarsely ground black pepper. Heat a non-stick griddle pan until very hot. Add the steaks to the grill pan and sear for 2 minutes on each side for medium rare, or 1–2 minutes longer according to taste. Set aside to rest.

2 Heat the remaining olive oil in a large shallow pan, add the onions and cook over a gentle heat for 5 minutes until beginning to soften. Add the curry paste to the pan and stir well. Cover and steam-fry for 5 minutes over a medium heat, stirring occasionally. Stir in the ginger and cook for 2 minutes.

3 Add the stock and chick peas to the pan, stir well and bring to the boil. Simmer for 10 minutes. Stir in the spring greens, cover and cook for a further minute.

4 Slice the steaks into thin strips on the diagonal and stir into the curry. Heat through for 1 minute and season to taste before serving.

a little meat goes a long way

For most people, red meat is one of the main sources of protein and a good source of iron. But you don't need to consume as much as you may think. An average adult needs just 75g (3oz) of protein per day – that is about as much as you can hold in the palm of your hand. So the trick is to buy smaller amounts of the best quality meat.

Choose the leanest cuts, such as pork loin, lamb fillet and beef sirloin or fillet, and trim away any fat. Look for very lean beef mince and bind it with an egg white and a dash of Worcestershire sauce to make your own burgers – then you'll know exactly what's in them! Lean cuts of meat are ideal griddled, grilled, stir- or steam-fried, and oven roasted. Use meat as a flavouring rather than the main ingredient in a dish, by combining it with lots of vegetables or salad, and you will appreciate its flavour and goodness in the best possible way. Each of the following recipes serves 4.

▲ **pork meatballs with smoked goulash sauce**
Mix 350g (12oz) lean pork mince, 100g (3½oz) grated carrot, zest of 2 lemons, 50g (2oz) diced sun-dried tomatoes, 2 tbsp chopped chives, 75g (3oz) fresh white breadcrumbs, pepper and 1 medium egg white. Shape into 12 balls. Bake at 200°C, gas 6 for 20 minutes. Sauté 2 diced aubergines in 1 tbsp oil for 5 minutes. Add 2 tsp smoked paprika and cook for 30 seconds. Stir in 350g (12oz) tub fresh tomato sauce and 200ml (7fl oz) red wine; simmer for 5 minutes. Serve with the meatballs.

fillet steak salad with hot green sauce

Toss 4 red onions, in wedges, in 1 tbsp olive oil and bake at 200°C, gas 6 for 35 minutes. Sear a 225g (8oz) end of tail fillet on a smoking hot non-stick griddle pan all over for 4–5 minutes, or to taste. Rest for 5 minutes. Toss onions with 400g can rinsed green lentils, 250g (9oz) watercress, 1 tbsp olive oil and pepper. Mix 1 tbsp wasabi paste with 7 tbsp yogurt. Thinly slice the steak and serve on the salad. Top with wasabi dressing.

sticky beef and pak choi stir-fry

Cook 250g (9oz) fine egg noodles. Heat 2 tsp groundnut oil in a non-stick wok and stir-fry 225g (8oz) sirloin steak strips over high heat for 2 minutes. Add 1 bunch finely chopped spring onions, 2 chopped red peppers, 2 crushed garlic cloves and 300g (11oz) shredded pak choi. Stir-fry for 1 minute. Stir in 4 tbsp plum sauce and 2 tbsp dry sherry; cook for 1 minute. Drain the noodles and toss with 2 tsp sesame oil. Serve the peppered beef on lettuce, scattered with the hot noodles.

▲ lamb with nectarine and cumin cous cous

Brush 4 x 140g (4½oz) lamb neck fillets with 2 tsp olive oil and roll in cracked pepper. Soak 225g (8oz) cous cous in 250ml (8fl oz) boiling water for 5 minutes. Fork through 3 tbsp extra virgin olive oil, juice of 1 lemon, pepper and 2 tsp toasted cumin seeds, then add 2 chopped nectarines and 20g (¾oz) chopped coriander. Heat a non-stick griddle pan until smoking. Cook the lamb fillets for 6–7 minutes, turning to brown evenly. Rest for 5 minutes, then slice thinly. Serve with the cous cous.

red Thai pork with green beans

For this simple aromatic curry, lean pork tenderloin is flavoured with Thai red curry paste and cooked in tomato passata with French beans. Serve with Thai fragrant rice, and a good dollop of cooling natural yogurt.

SERVES 4

2 teaspoons olive oil
1 red onion, peeled and finely chopped
225g (8oz) pork tenderloin
2 tablespoons Thai red curry paste
500g carton passata
1 teaspoon sugar
350g (12oz) French beans, topped and tailed
freshly ground black pepper
coriander or small basil leaves, to garnish

1   Heat the olive oil in a large shallow pan, add the chopped red onion and cook over a gentle heat for 10 minutes until soft and golden.

2   Meanwhile, cut the pork into 5mm (¼ inch) pieces. Turn up the heat under the pan to high, add the pork and cook, stirring, for 2 minutes until evenly coloured.

3   Stir in the Thai curry paste and cook for 1 minute. Pour in the passata, add the sugar and stir well. Bring to the boil, lower the heat and gently simmer for 8 minutes.

4   Meanwhile, blanch the French beans in boiling water for 1 minute, then drain and refresh under cold water; drain again and cut into short lengths. Add the beans to the curry and cook for a further minute.

5   Season with pepper to taste. Scatter coriander or basil leaves over the curry and serve accompanied by Thai fragrant rice, and yogurt if you like.

pork koftas with roasted red pepper salad

These spiced, lean pork skewers are served on a mouthwatering salad of roasted peppers and rocket, with a piquant sauce. Red peppers are one of the best sources of vitamin C.

SERVES 4

3 large red peppers, halved, cored and deseeded

2 tablespoons olive oil

1 onion, peeled and finely chopped

1 teaspoon cayenne pepper

2 teaspoons ground cumin

2 teaspoons ground coriander

450g (1lb) lean pork mince

1 egg white

1/2 bunch of flat leaf parsley, roughly chopped

100g (3 1/2 oz) rocket leaves

freshly ground black pepper

FOR THE SAUCE:

200g (7oz) Greek yogurt

1 garlic clove, peeled and crushed

50g (2oz) black and green olives, pitted and chopped

1/2 bunch of flat leaf parsley, roughly chopped

squeeze of lemon juice

1   Preheat oven to 200°C (fan oven 180°C), gas mark 6. Cut each pepper half into 4 strips, place on a roasting tray and drizzle with 1 tablespoon oil. Roast for 35–40 minutes until softened and lightly charred.

2   Meanwhile, heat the remaining olive oil in a pan. Add the onion and cook for 5–6 minutes until softened. Add the spices and cook for a further minute. Transfer to a large bowl and allow to cool for 5 minutes. Add the pork mince, egg white, parsley and plenty of black pepper. Mix thoroughly.

3   Preheat the grill to medium-high. Divide the pork mixture into eight and shape each into a thick sausage. Push the sharp end of a pre-soaked bamboo skewer through the length of each sausage and place on a grill pan. Grill the koftas for about 6 minutes, turning occasionally, until cooked through.

4   Meanwhile, combine the sauce ingredients in a bowl; season with pepper. Toss the roasted peppers with the rocket and divide between four plates. Top with the koftas, add a spoonful of sauce and serve.

pork and prune tagine style

This quick version of a Moroccan style stew is subtly spiced with harissa, a spice mix of chillies, coriander and caraway that features strongly in Middle Eastern cooking. Carrots and prunes give the dish a hint of sweetness and added nutrients. Carrots are, of course, rich in beta-carotene, the plant form of vitamin A, while prunes are a good source of potassium, iron and fibre.

SERVES 4

450g (1lb) pork tenderloin, trimmed
2 tablespoons harissa paste
1 tablespoon olive oil
450ml (³/₄ pint) vegetable stock
1 onion, peeled and thinly sliced
grated zest and juice of 1 orange
4 carrots, peeled and cut into chunks on
   the diagonal
175g (6oz) ready-to-eat prunes
1 cinnamon stick
2 tablespoons chopped coriander leaves
freshly ground black pepper

1   Cut the pork tenderloin into 1cm (½ inch) rounds and place in a bowl. Add the harissa paste and toss well to coat evenly.

2   Heat the olive oil in a large shallow pan, add the pork and cook for 1 minute on each side or until golden. Remove with a slotted spoon and set aside.

3   Add 4 tablespoons of the stock and the onion to the pan, cover and steam-fry over a medium heat for 5 minutes, stirring occasionally, until softened and golden.

4   Stir in the orange zest and juice, together with the remaining stock. Return the pork to the pan and add the carrots, prunes and cinnamon stick. Bring to the boil, then lower the heat and simmer for 15–20 minutes.

5   Season to taste with black pepper and scatter over chopped coriander leaves. Serve the tagine with cous cous or basmati rice.

gammon with griddled pineapple and baby corn

Here is a healthy, fresh twist to an old favourite. Lean gammon steaks or pork loin steaks are marinated in honey and orange juice, char-grilled and served with griddled fresh pineapple and baby corn. The marinade is spiked with red chilli and drizzled over the gammon to serve. An excellent recipe to boost your vitamin levels and contribute to your five-a-day fruit and veg.

SERVES 4

4 gammon steaks or pork loin steaks, each
*   150g (5oz)*
juice of 2 oranges
1 tablespoon thin honey
1/2 bunch of spring onions, trimmed and
*   finely chopped*
1 small pineapple
200g (7oz) baby corn
2 teaspoons olive oil
1 red chilli, deseeded and finely chopped
freshly ground black pepper

1 Place the gammon steaks in a non-metallic dish, drizzle over the orange juice and honey, then add the spring onions and season well with black pepper. Set aside for 15 minutes.

2 Cut away the skin from the pineapple, then quarter and remove the core from each wedge. Heat a non-stick griddle pan until really hot. Cook the pineapple wedges and baby corn for 2 minutes each side or until slightly charred on the outside. Remove from the pan and keep warm.

3 Heat the olive oil in the griddle pan. Remove the gammon steaks from the marinade, reserving the liquid, and add to the pan. Cook for 3–4 minutes on each side, then transfer to warm serving plates.

4 Pour the reserved marinade into the pan and allow to bubble over a medium heat for 1 minute. Stir in the chilli and season to taste. Arrange the pineapple and baby corn alongside the gammon. Drizzle the hot dressing over and serve straightaway.

6 pasta and rice

roasted butternut farfalle

Butternut squash and red onion wedges are roasted together until caramelised and sweet, then teamed with rocket, pasta and toasted pine nuts for a simple, yet stunning and satisfying meal. Winter squash varieties, such as butternut, contain useful amounts of vitamin A.

SERVES 4

1 large butternut squash, peeled, halved and
  deseeded
2 large red onions, peeled and cut into thin
  wedges
2 tablespoons olive oil
350g (12oz) dried farfalle, or other pasta shapes
50g (2oz) pine nuts, lightly toasted
50g (2oz) wild rocket
freshly ground black pepper
balsamic vinegar, to drizzle

1   Preheat the oven to 200°C (fan oven 180°C), gas mark 6. Cut the butternut squash into 2.5cm (1 inch) pieces and place in a large roasting tin with the red onions. Drizzle with the olive oil and season with black pepper. Roast for 40–45 minutes until the vegetables are tender and slightly caramelised.

2   About 10 minutes before the end of the roasting time, cook the pasta in a large pan of boiling water according to the packet instructions, until *al dente* (cooked but with a bite).

3   Drain the pasta, reserving 2 tablespoons of the cooking water, then return to the pan. Add the roasted vegetables, pine nuts and rocket with the reserved water. Toss to mix and season with plenty of black pepper. Pile on to warm serving plates, drizzle with a little balsamic vinegar and serve.

spaghetti rosti with tuna

This is a novel way of serving spaghetti, which is always a favourite in our home. Buy tuna canned in spring water rather than oil or brine. It's an excellent source of protein, though it doesn't provide the beneficial omega-3 fatty acids that fresh tuna offers, because these are lost in the canning process. Serve the rosti warm, cold or even cut into wedges and packed into lunchboxes.

SERVES 4–6

225g (8oz) dried spaghetti
1 tablespoon olive oil
1 onion, peeled and finely chopped
1 garlic clove, peeled and crushed

5 eggs, beaten
2 x 160g cans yellow fin tuna in spring water,
  drained and flaked
40g (1½oz) mature Cheddar cheese, grated
freshly ground black pepper

1 Cook the spaghetti in a large pan of boiling water for 8–10 minutes or until *al dente* (cooked but with a bite). Drain, rinse under cold running water, drain well and place in a large bowl.

2 Meanwhile, heat the olive oil in a large non-stick frying pan (suitable for use under the grill). Add the onion and cook for 5 minutes, then stir in the garlic and cook for a further minute. Add to the cooked pasta with the beaten eggs and tuna and toss to mix, seasoning well.

3 Preheat the grill. Arrange the spaghetti mixture evenly in the frying pan and scatter over the cheese. Continue to cook on the hob for 10 minutes or until the eggs are almost set.

4 Place under the grill for 3–4 minutes or until just set and golden on top. Slide the rosti out of the pan on to a board. Cut into wedges and serve with roasted vine tomatoes or salad leaves.

lemon and haddock penne bake

Juicy flakes of natural smoked haddock, penne pasta and broccoli are baked in a creamy lemon sauce beneath a crispy, cheesy crumb topping. This bake is a great way to include broccoli, an excellent source of vitamin C and antioxidants that may help to reduce the risk of certain cancers.

SERVES 4

300g (11oz) dried penne or other pasta shapes
250g (9oz) broccoli florets
450g (1lb) natural smoked haddock fillet
450ml (3/4 pint) semi-skimmed milk
25g (1oz) butter
1 tablespoon plain flour
grated zest and juice of 1/2 lemon
40g (11/2oz) mature Cheddar cheese, grated
5 tablespoons fresh white breadcrumbs
freshly ground black pepper

1 Preheat the oven to 200°C (fan oven 180°C), gas mark 6. Cook the pasta in a large pan of boiling water according to the packet instructions, until *al dente* (cooked but with a bite). Blanch the broccoli florets in boiling water for 2 minutes, then drain and refresh in cold water.

2 Place the smoked haddock fillet in a shallow pan, pour over the milk and cover with a circle of greaseproof paper. Bring to a simmer and poach gently for 3–4 minutes. Remove the smoked haddock to a plate, reserving the milk.

3 Melt the butter in a small pan, stir in the flour and cook over a gentle heat for 2 minutes. Slowly whisk in the reserved milk and cook for 5 minutes. Add the lemon zest and juice, and season the sauce with pepper to taste.

4 Drain the pasta as soon as it is cooked. Roughly flake the haddock and mix with the pasta and broccoli florets. Place in a large gratin dish and pour over the sauce.

5 Mix together the Cheddar cheese and breadcrumbs, then scatter over the top. Bake in the oven for 10 minutes or until bubbling hot and golden. Serve immediately, accompanied by a tomato salad.

boston bean and sausage macaroni

Now that you can buy so many different types of canned beans, soaking and slow-cooking dried pulses is becoming a thing of the past. Make sure you use good quality sausages for this American style dish, as they'll be less fatty and more flavoursome. Finish with shavings of mature Cheddar and peppery rocket leaves – the stronger the cheese, the less you need to provide flavour.

SERVES 4

4 good quality sausages
175g (6oz) dried macaroni
500g carton passata
40g (1¹/₂oz) brown sugar
3 tablespoons tomato ketchup
3 tablespoons white wine vinegar
dash of Worcestershire sauce
400g can pinto beans, drained and rinsed
400g can haricot beans, drained and rinsed
good handful of rocket leaves
40g (1¹/₂oz) mature Cheddar cheese, pared
  into shavings
freshly ground black pepper

1 Preheat the oven to 200°C (fan oven 180°C), gas mark 6. Preheat the grill. Place the sausages on the grill pan or a baking tray and cook under the grill for 12–15 minutes, turning frequently, until browned all over and cooked through.

2 Cook the macaroni in a large pan of boiling water according to the packet instructions, until *al dente* (cooked but with a bite).

3 Meanwhile, place the passata, sugar, tomato ketchup, wine vinegar and Worcestershire sauce in a pan. Stir together, then add the pinto and haricot beans and simmer for 10 minutes.

4 Drain the macaroni and add to the beans. Cut each sausage into 4 chunky slices and stir into the bean mixture, then season to taste. Spoon into an ovenproof gratin dish and place in the oven for 8–10 minutes until piping hot. Just before serving, scatter over the rocket leaves and cheese shavings.

simply dressed pasta

Endlessly versatile, pasta is a great staple and carrier of flavours, and it is not fattening unless, of course, you dress it to be so. It is essentially an energy food – high in beneficial complex carbohydrate, low in fat and a useful source of protein. Dried pasta is often considered superior to the bought fresh equivalent and, if made from 100% durum wheat, it is slightly higher in protein. There is an extraordinary range of shapes, sizes and colours to choose from.

For perfect results, cook your pasta completely immersed in the largest pan of boiling water, without a lid. Use the time given on the packet as a guide, but keep tasting towards the end of cooking. The pasta is ready when it's *al dente* or 'firm to the tooth' – not hard and chalky, and not soggy. Stop cooking by tipping a cup of cold water into the pan and drain quickly, leaving a little water on the pasta. Try the following original ideas for pasta – each serves 4.

▲ chillied tenderstem broccoli

Cook 350g (12oz) rigatoni in boiling water until *al dente*. Trim 350g (12oz) long stem broccoli, cut into long florets and steam for 4 minutes or until *al dente*. Drain the cooked pasta and toss with the broccoli, 2 deseeded and finely diced red chillies, a squeeze of lemon juice and 2 tbsp extra virgin olive oil. Grind over lots of black pepper and serve straightaway.

▼ roasted tomato and olive sauce

Put 250g (9oz) each cherry tomatoes and baby plum tomatoes into a roasting tin. Add 175g (6oz) each black and green olives, pitted and sliced, a pinch of sugar, 2 tbsp olive oil and plenty of black pepper. Roast at 200°C, gas 6 for 20–25 minutes. Meanwhile, cook 350g (12oz) tagliatelle in a large pan of boiling water until *al dente*. Drain well and toss with the roasted tomato sauce, mixing in all the pan juices.

Moroccan dressed chick peas

Heat 2 tsp olive oil in a pan, stir in 1 thinly sliced red onion and steam-fry for 5 minutes. Stir in 2 tbsp harissa paste, 6 tbsp white wine and a 400g can chopped tomatoes. Simmer gently for 10 minutes. Add a 400g can drained chick peas and heat through. Season to taste. Meanwhile, cook 350g (12oz) dried penne or other pasta shapes in plenty of boiling water for 8–10 minutes or until *al dente*. Drain the pasta and return to the pan. Toss with the chick pea sauce and serve.

▲ pea pesto with ricotta and ham

Cook 350g (12oz) pasta spirals in boiling water until *al dente*. Cook 225g (8oz) frozen petit pois in boiling water for 3 minutes then drain, reserving 125ml (4fl oz) liquid. In a food processor, whiz the peas and reserved liquid with 5 tbsp basil leaves, 125g (4oz) ricotta cheese, 2 tsp lemon juice and 1 crushed garlic clove until fairly smooth; add pepper to taste. Gently heat the pea pesto. Drain the pasta and toss with the pesto. Serve topped with wafer-thin slices of dry cured ham and basil.

oriental rice with sugar snaps and shiitake mushrooms

This sticky risotto, infused with Japanese flavours, is a tasty low-fat alternative to a traditional Italian risotto. Furikake seasoning is made from nutritious black and white sesame seeds and seaweed, and has a delicious nutty flavour. You buy furikake in a jar – look for it near the soy sauce or seaweed products.

Illustrated on previous page

SERVES 4

2 sachets instant miso soup powder
1 tablespoon olive oil
5cm (2 inch) piece fresh root ginger, peeled and
  finely chopped
1 garlic clove, peeled and crushed
1 small red chilli, deseeded and finely chopped
1/2 bunch of spring onions, trimmed and chopped
225g (8oz) arborio rice
350g (12oz) sugar snap peas, trimmed
250g (9oz) shiitake mushrooms, sliced
2 tablespoons Japanese furikake seasoning
2 teaspoons mirin
freshly ground black pepper
coriander sprigs, to garnish

1 Mix the miso powder with 900ml (1 1/2 pints) boiling water in a saucepan and keep at a gentle simmer over a low heat.

2 Heat 1/2 tablespoon olive oil in a pan over a medium heat, add the ginger, garlic, chilli and spring onions, and cook for 1 minute. Stir in the rice.

3 Keeping the rice over a medium heat, add the miso, a ladleful at a time, stirring constantly and making sure each addition is absorbed before adding more (this will take approximately 20 minutes). The rice is cooked when it looks thick and creamy, but still retains a bite. Season to taste.

4 Heat the remaining olive oil in a non-stick wok or large non-stick frying pan. Add the sugar snap peas and mushrooms and stir-fry for 2–3 minutes. Stir in the furikake seasoning and mirin, and cook for a further 30 seconds.

5 Spoon the rice into warm serving bowls, and add the stir-fried sugar snaps and mushrooms. Garnish with coriander sprigs and serve immediately.

green rice soubise

Wholemeal rice contains more fibre than white rice but it does take longer to cook. Fortunately, this lemony wholemeal rice dish is baked, so once it's in the oven you can forget about it. Onions are one of the richest sources of flavonoids – antioxidants that help our immune system. This simple dish is finished with a scattering of creamy ricotta, a versatile low-fat whey cheese.

SERVES 4

1 tablespoon olive oil
2 onions, peeled and finely chopped
2 garlic cloves, peeled and crushed
350g (12oz) short-grain American easy-cook
   brown rice, rinsed
1 unwaxed lemon, cut into 4 wedges
1.2 litres (2 pints) vegetable stock
250g (9oz) broccoli florets
175g (6oz) frozen peas, thawed
1 bunch of spring onions, trimmed and chopped
125g (4oz) ricotta cheese
2 tablespoons torn basil
freshly ground black pepper

1   Preheat the oven to 200°C (fan oven 180°C), gas mark 6. Heat the olive oil in a large shallow ovenproof pan, add the onions and cook over a medium heat for 5 minutes, stirring occasionally. Add the garlic and cook for a further 2 minutes until the onions are softened and golden.

2   Add the rice and lemon wedges, then stir well. Pour in the stock, bring to the boil and cover with foil. Cook in the oven for 45–50 minutes. In the meantime, blanch the broccoli in boiling water for 2–3 minutes, then drain and refresh under cold running water.

3   Remove the rice dish from oven and stir in the broccoli, peas and spring onions. Season well and crumble the ricotta on top. Bake, uncovered, for a further 6–8 minutes or until the rice is tender and most of the liquid has been absorbed. Scatter over the basil and serve straightaway.

jambalaya

Red rice comes from the Camargue region of Southern France. It has a good flavour, nutty texture and a distinctive colour. In this paella-style dish, I have cooked the rice separately to speed things up. The peppers are a good source of beta-carotene, the plant form of vitamin A, which may help to reduce the risk of some forms of cancer and heart disease. The main flavouring is pimenton, a smoked sweet paprika, which gives this dish a certain edge.

SERVES 4

2 skinless chicken breast fillets, each about
    150g (5oz)
1 each red, yellow and orange peppers
350g (12oz) Camargue red rice
80g packet sliced chorizo sausage
1 tablespoon olive oil
1 red onion, peeled and cut into 8 wedges

2 garlic cloves, peeled and crushed
1¹/₂ teaspoons smoked paprika
pinch of ground cloves
3 bay leaves
400g can chopped tomatoes
200ml (7fl oz) vegetable stock
freshly ground black pepper

1 Cut the chicken into 2.5cm (1 inch) pieces. Halve, core and deseed the peppers, then chop roughly. Cook the rice in a pan of boiling water according to the packet instructions.

2 Meanwhile, heat a large shallow pan, add the chorizo slices and cook for 30 seconds on each side until golden. Remove with a slotted spoon and set aside. Add the chicken pieces to the pan and sauté for 10 minutes until golden all over. Remove from the pan and drain on kitchen paper.

3 Add the olive oil to the pan. Add the red onion and peppers and cook for 5 minutes or until the vegetables are lightly golden. Stir in the garlic, smoked paprika, cloves and bay leaves. Cook for 1 minute.

4 Stir in the drained, cooked rice, chorizo and chicken. Add the tomatoes and stock, and bring to the boil. Simmer for 8–10 minutes or until most of the liquid has been absorbed. Season to taste and serve.

baked chicken and thyme risotto

This oven-baked chicken risotto doesn't require constant stirring, but the result is still creamy and flavoursome. It is rich in protein, carbohydrates and wheat-free. Dried porcini mushrooms lend a superb intense flavour that combines well with the garlic and thyme.

SERVES 4

25g (1oz) dried porcini mushrooms
4 skinless chicken thigh fillets
2 garlic cloves, peeled and crushed
2 teaspoons thyme leaves, plus extra to garnish
1 tablespoon olive oil
1 large onion, peeled and finely chopped
1 litre (1¾ pints) vegetable stock
350g (12oz) arborio rice
100ml (3½fl oz) white wine
freshly ground black pepper

1   Put the dried mushrooms in a bowl, pour over warm water to cover and leave to soak for about 30 minutes. Preheat the oven to 190°C (fan oven 170°C), gas mark 5.

2   With a small sharp knife, slash the chicken thighs on the diagonal, just cutting through the flesh. Rub them all over with the garlic and thyme, then season with pepper.

3   Heat the olive oil in a large shallow ovenproof pan and cook the chicken for 2–3 minutes on each side until golden. Remove from the pan and set aside.

4   Add the onion to the pan with a splash of stock and cook gently for 5 minutes or until softened. Stir in the rice and stir continuously for 1 minute. Add the drained mushrooms and cook for a further minute. Pour in the wine and cook for 2 minutes until it has evaporated.

5   Add the stock and bring to the boil. Season well. Place the chicken thighs on top of the rice. Cover with a lid and cook in the oven for 20–25 minutes until the rice is just cooked and all the stock has been absorbed. Scatter over extra thyme leaves, then serve.

crab and salmon kedgeree

This modern version of an old English breakfast dish is surprisingly spiced with Thai green curry paste. Crab tastes deliciously different in the kedgeree, while roasted salmon strips provide an attractive topping. A cooling carrot and coriander raita is the ideal accompaniment.

SERVES 4

2 teaspoons olive oil
1 onion, peeled and finely chopped
2 tablespoons Thai green curry paste
2 tablespoons mango chutney
150ml (¼ pint) white wine
300ml (½ pint) vegetable stock
350g (12oz) basmati rice, rinsed
350g (12oz) boneless, skinless salmon fillet
170g can white crabmeat, drained

FOR THE RAITA:
200g (7oz) natural yogurt
1 small carrot, peeled and grated
20g (¾oz) coriander leaves, chopped
freshly ground black pepper

1 Preheat the oven to 200°C (fan oven 180°C), gas mark 6. Heat the olive oil in a pan, stir in the onion and steam-fry for 10 minutes or until soft and golden. Stir in the curry paste and mango chutney and cook for 1 minute. Pour in the wine and stock, then cook until reduced to about 250ml (8fl oz).

2 Meanwhile, cook the rice according to the packet instructions. Cut the salmon into 8 strips lengthways and place on a non-stick baking tray. Bake in the oven for 5–7 minutes until just cooked.

3 Mix all the ingredients for the raita together in a bowl and season well with black pepper.

4 Drain the rice and gently toss with the reduced curry paste mixture, then fork through the crabmeat. Spoon the kedgeree on to warm serving plates, top with the salmon strips and serve immediately, with the carrot and coriander raita.

7 salads and vegetables

cashew nut and rice noodle salad

These rice noodles are great for anyone on a wheat-free diet and they're so quick to cook. Toast the cashew nuts to give maximum flavour to the dressing, keeping an eye on them as they quickly scorch and acquire a bitter taste. Cashew nuts contain protein, minerals, especially magnesium, and some B vitamins. Carrot ribbons are an attractive addition – cucumber and courgette ribbons look good in salads too.

SERVES 4

50g (2oz) cashew nuts
2 medium carrots, peeled
20g (³/₄oz) coriander
2 tablespoons light soy sauce
juice of 1 large orange
3 garlic cloves, peeled and crushed
2 tablespoons grapeseed oil
250g (9oz) rice noodles, cooked
1 bunch of radishes, trimmed and sliced
125g (4oz) bean sprouts
freshly ground black pepper

1 Place the cashew nuts in a small dry frying pan over a medium heat and toast for about 3 minutes, shaking the pan constantly, until an even golden colour. Set aside to cool slightly.

2 Using a swivel vegetable peeler, pare along the length of the carrots to make long, thin ribbons and set aside.

3 Set aside a handful of coriander sprigs. Put the rest into a food processor with the toasted cashew nuts, soy sauce, orange juice, garlic and grapeseed oil. Whiz until fairly smooth, then season to taste.

4 Toss the noodles, carrot ribbons, radishes and bean sprouts together. Pour over the dressing and toss well to coat evenly. Scatter over the reserved coriander to serve.

harissa beefsteak tomatoes with tabbouleh

Tabbouleh is a fragrant Middle Eastern salad made with nutty bulghar wheat, lemon juice, olive oil and lots of freshly chopped mint and parsley. Here it is served with oven-roasted tomatoes, spiked with harissa paste. Pine nuts, high in essential fatty acids, give this dish some added protein, making it a complete meal for vegetarians.

SERVES 4

225g (8oz) bulghar wheat

4 beefsteak tomatoes, halved

2 tablespoons harissa paste

2 tablespoons extra virgin olive oil, plus extra
  to drizzle

juice of 1 lemon

20g (¾oz) mint, chopped

20g (¾oz) flat leaf parsley, chopped

75g (3oz) pine nuts, toasted

freshly ground black pepper

TO SERVE:

natural yogurt

1   Preheat the oven to 220°C (fan oven 200°C), gas mark 7. Put the bulghar wheat in a bowl and add cold water to just cover. Set aside for 30 minutes or until the water has been absorbed.

2   Place the tomatoes, cut-side up, on a baking tray and spread with the harissa paste. Roast in the oven for 10–12 minutes or until just softened but still holding their shape.

3   Meanwhile, toss the bulghar wheat with the olive oil, lemon juice, chopped mint and parsley. Season to taste.

4   Spoon the tabbouleh on to four plates and top each serving with two roasted tomato halves. Scatter over the toasted pine nuts and drizzle with a little extra virgin olive oil. Serve with yogurt.

guacamole and bean salad on toasted pitta

Chunky guacamole, made from nutrient-rich avocados, partners a Mexican style bean and watercress salad that's rich in fibre and iron. Toasted pitta bread is the ideal accompaniment.

SERVES 4

2 ripe avocados

juice of 1 lime

2 shallots, peeled and finely chopped

10 cherry tomatoes, quartered

1 red chilli, deseeded and finely chopped

2 garlic cloves, peeled and crushed

2 tablespoons extra virgin olive oil

400g can kidney beans, drained and rinsed

75g (3oz) bag ready-prepared watercress

6 pitta breads, toasted

freshly ground black pepper

1   Halve, stone and peel the avocados, then cut into 1cm (½ inch) cubes. Place in a bowl and pour over the lime juice. Add the shallots, tomatoes, chilli, 1 garlic clove and 1 tablespoon olive oil, and gently mix together. Season with black pepper.

2   Toss the kidney beans with the remaining garlic and olive oil, then toss in the watercress and season well. Spoon on to toasted pitta breads and top with the chunky guacamole.

warm peppered goat's cheese salad

Goat's cheese has a sharp, gutsy flavour, so a little goes a long way. Here it is coated in black pepper, then griddled until golden and served on salad leaves with an unusual red pepper and lentil dressing.

SERVES 4

2 x 100g (3½oz) goat's cheese with rind

1 tablespoon freshly ground black pepper

2 tablespoons cooked Puy lentils

1 small red pepper, deseeded and finely diced

3 tablespoons extra virgin olive oil

juice of ½ lemon

150g (5oz) baby salad leaves

1   Cut each cheese in half horizontally and coat all over with the pepper, pressing to adhere. Heat a non-stick griddle pan until hot. Add the peppered cheese, cut-side down, and griddle for 2 minutes or until coloured and crusty. Turn over and cook for a further 1 minute or until the cheese is soft but still retaining its shape.

2   Meanwhile, mix together the lentils, red pepper, olive oil and lemon juice in a small bowl; season well. Arrange the salad leaves on serving plates, top with the griddled goat's cheese and spoon over the dressing to serve.

warm potato and egg salad

This is a lovely fresh combination of colourful ingredients. Tossing the baby new potatoes in the mustard dressing while they are still hot encourages them to soak up all the flavours. Potatoes are a useful source of vitamin C, potassium and fibre. The salad is topped with soft-boiled eggs and sprinkled with mustard and cress – one of my favourite salad items.

SERVES 4

575g (1¼lb) baby new potatoes, scrubbed
225g (8oz) green beans, trimmed and halved
250g (9oz) cherry tomatoes, halved
4 eggs
2 punnets mustard and cress, trimmed

FOR THE DRESSING:

2 teaspoons Dijon mustard
1 tablespoon white wine vinegar
1 shallot, peeled and finely chopped
1 garlic clove, peeled and crushed
3 tablespoons extra virgin olive oil
freshly ground black pepper

1   Place the baby potatoes in a pan of cold water, bring to the boil and simmer for 20 minutes or until just tender.

2   Meanwhile, make the dressing. Whisk the Dijon mustard, wine vinegar, shallot, garlic and olive oil together in a bowl and season to taste.

3   Drain the potatoes and toss them in the dressing. Set aside to cool for 5 minutes. Blanch the green beans in boiling water for 1 minute, then drain and refresh under cold running water; drain well. Add the beans and tomatoes to the potatoes and toss to mix.

4   Meanwhile, place the eggs in a pan with enough boiling water to cover and boil gently for 2 minutes. Put the eggs under running cold water, then remove and very carefully peel them.

5   To serve, spoon the salad into bowls, top each serving with a soft-boiled egg and scatter over mustard and cress. Serve immediately.

griddled pear, chicken and endive salad

Griddled, sliced pears complement bitter salad leaves, tangy Roquefort and cooked chicken to delicious effect. Toasted walnuts provide a crunchy contrast and enhance the nutrient value – they are rich in essential fatty acids and a useful source of protein, B vitamins, vitamin E and minerals. Chicken is full of protein – buy organic or free-range for the healthiest option.

SERVES 4

2 large, ripe William or Comice pears
200g bag curly endive (frisé) and radicchio salad
275g (10oz) cooked chicken breast
50g (2oz) walnuts, toasted
50g (2oz) Roquefort cheese, crumbled

FOR THE DRESSING:

2 tablespoons extra virgin olive oil
2 tablespoons balsamic vinegar
freshly ground black pepper

1 Halve, quarter, core and thickly slice the pears. Heat a non-stick griddle pan until very hot. Add the pear slices and griddle for 1 minute on each side or until lightly charred. Remove and set aside.

2 For the dressing, whisk the olive oil and balsamic vinegar together in a small bowl. Season with pepper to taste.

3 Tear the chicken into bite-sized pieces. Arrange the salad leaves on four serving plates and top with the chicken, pears, toasted walnuts and crumbled blue cheese. Drizzle the dressing over the salad and grind over a little extra black pepper. Serve with Granary bread.

melon, roasted pepper and ham salad

A colourful summer salad of ripe, juicy melon and roasted orange peppers topped with honey roast ham, tangy Pecorino cheese and rocket. Pecorino is an Italian sheep's milk cheese and is rich in protein and calcium.

Illustrated on previous page

SERVES 4

3 large orange peppers
2 teaspoons olive oil
1 small ripe Charentais or Galia melon
100g (3¹/₂oz) rocket leaves

125g (4oz) wafer-thin honey roast ham slices
50g (2oz) Pecorino cheese, crumbled
freshly ground black pepper
extra virgin olive oil, to drizzle

1 Preheat the oven to 220°C (fan oven 200°C), gas mark 7. Quarter, core and deseed the peppers, then place in a roasting tin and drizzle with the olive oil. Roast for 20–25 minutes. Set aside to cool.

2 Cut the melon in half and scoop out the seeds. Cut each half into 4 wedges. Arrange the rocket on serving plates and top with the melon, roasted peppers and ham. Scatter over the cheese and finish with a generous grinding of black pepper and a little drizzle of extra virgin olive oil.

mango crab salad

Fragrant mango, fresh crab, crisp salad leaves and a lime pickle mayonnaise make a healthy salad with a difference. Mango is a rich in vitamins C, A and E. Like all shellfish, crab is a good source of protein, B vitamins and some minerals, including zinc.

SERVES 4

1 Cos lettuce, trimmed
1 cucumber
1 small ripe mango
250g (9oz) fresh brown crabmeat
350g (12oz) fresh white crabmeat
1 lime, cut into wedges

FOR THE DRESSING:
3 tablespoons low-fat mayonnaise
6 tablespoons natural yogurt
2 tablespoons hot lime pickle

1 Tear the Cos lettuce leaves into pieces. Peel, halve, deseed and slice the cucumber on the diagonal. Peel, halve and slice the mango away from the stone. Arrange these ingredients on a large platter, or individual plates.

2 Place a mound of brown crabmeat in the centre and top with the fresh white crabmeat. Mix the dressing ingredients together in a bowl. Serve the crab salad with the lime pickle mayonnaise, lime wedges and some good brown bread.

spinach and Parmesan polenta bake

If you have never used polenta before, you will be amazed at how easy it is to cook with. Here, I've flavoured it with nutrient-rich spinach, Parmesan and nutmeg, then baked it as a savoury pudding. This is delicious served with a simple plum tomato salad.

SERVES 4

2 teaspoons olive oil
1 onion, peeled and finely chopped
400ml (14fl oz) semi-skimmed milk
125g (4oz) instant polenta
3 large eggs, separated
50g (2oz) Parmesan cheese, grated
1 teaspoon ground nutmeg
175g (6oz) baby spinach leaves, roughly chopped
freshly ground black pepper

FOR THE SALAD:

6 ripe plum tomatoes
splash of balsamic vinegar
1 bunch of basil leaves

1 Preheat the oven to 200°C (fan oven 180°C), gas mark 6. Lightly oil a 1.2 litre (2 pint) gratin dish.

2 Heat the olive oil in a pan, add the onion and gently cook for 10 minutes or until softened and golden brown. Pour in the milk and 300ml (½ pint) water, then bring to the boil.

3 Stir in the polenta, beat well until smooth and remove from heat. Beat in the egg yolks, Parmesan, nutmeg and spinach, then season generously.

4 Whisk the egg whites until they form soft peaks and gently fold into the polenta mixture. Spoon into the prepared dish. Bake for 20–25 minutes or until slightly puffed up and golden brown.

5 Meanwhile, thinly slice the plum tomatoes and arrange on a serving plate. Drizzle with the balsamic vinegar, scatter over the basil and grind over plenty of pepper. Serve with the polenta bake.

potatoes

Cooked with a new attitude, potatoes have a role in a healthy diet. They're rich in complex carbohydrate and contain useful amounts of fibre, Vitamin C and protein. Some nutrients are concentrated just under the skin, so scrub potatoes rather than peel them if possible.

Choosing from the many varieties can be bewildering. For crisp-skinned, fluffy jacket potatoes, I recommend large King Edwards. Bake for about 1 hour in a hot oven, turning halfway – don't be tempted to microwave. For perfect creamy mash, I opt for Desirée. Cut into pieces and boil for 15–20 minutes until tender, drain and mash with a little hot milk, a spoonful of yogurt and black pepper. For extra taste, add a touch of grainy mustard or horseradish. Charlotte and Anya are ideal salad potatoes – boil and dress with chopped herbs, or toss in a little olive oil and roast until crisp. For oven chips, I buy Maris Pipers – a great all rounder – for boiling, mashing and baking. Each of these recipes serves 4.

▲ **baked jackets with sesame and sunflower slaw**
Bake 4 large potatoes at 200°C, gas 6 for about 1 hour until tender, turning them over halfway through cooking. Meanwhile, mix together 1 tbsp soy sauce, 2 tbsp soured cream, 1 tbsp reduced-fat mayonnaise and 25g (1oz) each of toasted sunflower and sesame seeds. Toss this dressing with 3 peeled, grated carrots, 150g (5oz) bean sprouts and 4 chopped spring onions. Pile into the hot jacket potatoes and top with coriander leaves to serve.

potato and onion cakes

Scrub 3 medium potatoes, grate and dry well on kitchen paper. Mix with 1 finely sliced red onion, 2 tbsp olive oil, a little nutmeg and black pepper. Divide into 4 portions and press into thin rounds on a preheated non-stick baking tray. Bake at 200°C, gas 6 for 25–30 minutes or until golden. Serve on a salad of baby leaf spinach and grilled lean bacon with a drizzle of balsamic vinegar.

potato and leek broth with pesto greens

Heat ½ tbsp olive oil in a large pan. Add 2 chopped leeks, 1 peeled, chopped large sweet potato, 2 peeled, chopped medium potatoes and a bay leaf. Cover and cook for 10 minutes. Pour in 800ml (1⅓ pints) vegetable stock and a splash of white wine. Simmer for 15–20 minutes. Meanwhile cook 200g (7oz) shredded spring greens with 2 tbsp water in a covered wok for 2 minutes; stir in 1 tbsp pesto. Ladle the broth into bowls and top with the greens.

▲ roasted new potato salad with smoked trout

Toss 750g (1lb 10oz) baby new potatoes with black pepper and 1 tbsp olive oil. Roast at 190°C, gas 5 for 45 minutes or until tender. Mix together 2 tsp wholegrain mustard, 1 tsp Dijon mustard, 4 tbsp Greek yogurt, juice of ½ lemon, 1 tbsp water and ¼ tsp thin honey. Divide 2 large handfuls lamb's lettuce, 250g (9oz) halved, cooked baby beetroot, 75g (3oz) flaked smoked trout and the hot potatoes between plates and drizzle with the dressing.

vegetable hash with eggs

A mixed root vegetable rosti of potatoes, carrots and leeks – topped with protein-rich eggs – makes an appetising, healthy lunch or supper. Always buy free-range or organic eggs for taste and quality. For best results, use a good quality non-stick pan to fry the rosti.

SERVES 4

450g (1lb) Maris Piper or King Edward
*   potatoes, peeled*
2 tablespoons olive oil
2 leeks, trimmed and finely shredded
2 carrots, peeled and grated
4 small or medium eggs
1 tablespoon chopped flat leaf parsley
freshly ground black pepper

1   Grate the potatoes, then squeeze out as much liquid as possible with your hands and pat dry on kitchen paper. Preheat the grill.

2   Heat the olive oil in a large 23–25cm (9–10 inch) non-stick frying pan (suitable for use under the grill). Add the leeks and cook, stirring, for 2 minutes. Stir in the grated potatoes and carrots, then lightly spread out the mixture in the pan. Fry over a medium heat for 10 minutes until golden underneath.

3   Place the pan under the grill and cook for 5 minutes or until the rosti is golden on top. Remove from the grill and make four indentations in the surface of the rosti.

4   Crack the eggs into the indentations, grind over a little black pepper and scatter over the chopped parsley. Cover with a lid or baking sheet, place back on the hob over a medium heat and cook for 4–5 minutes or until eggs are cooked to your liking. Serve straightaway.

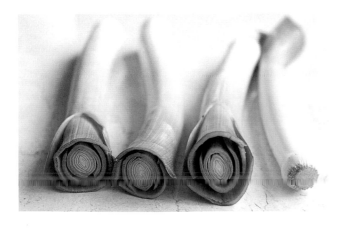

pak choi and noodle stir-fry

Chinese pak choi are particularly delicious in stir-fries and they are now widely available, though you could substitute spring greens or Savoy cabbage if you prefer. Stir-frying is one of the healthiest ways of cooking these vegetables as it helps to preserve their vitamin C – the least stable of all vitamins. Rather than wash mushrooms, simply wipe clean with damp kitchen paper.

SERVES 4

250g (9oz) thin egg noodles
2 tablespoons groundnut oil
250g (9oz) small chestnut mushrooms, halved or
  quartered if large
2 garlic cloves, peeled and crushed
2 red chillies, deseeded and finely chopped
3 pak choi, shredded
2 tablespoons soy sauce
2 tablespoons sweet chilli dipping sauce
freshly ground black pepper
coriander sprigs, to garnish

1 Cook the egg noodles in boiling water according to the packet instructions.

2 At the same time, cook the stir-fry. Heat the groundnut oil in a non-stick wok or large non-stick frying pan. Add the mushrooms and garlic and stir-fry for 1–2 minutes. Stir in the chillies and cook for 30 seconds. Add the pak choi and stir-fry for 1 minute.

3 Toss in the drained egg noodles, soy and chilli sauces, and season with pepper to taste. Heat through for 1 minute or until the noodles are piping hot. Divide between warm bowls, garnish with coriander and serve at once.

roasted Mediterranean vegetable crust

This impressive upside-down tart is very easy to make, using a ciabatta bread mix. Roasted aubergine, courgettes, red peppers, red onion and cherry tomatoes are baked under the ciabatta dough, then inverted and topped with crumbled feta to serve. Feta cheese is a sheep's milk cheese – useful for anyone with an intolerance to cow's milk protein.

SERVES 6

1 aubergine

2 courgettes, trimmed

2 red peppers, halved and deseeded

1 small red onion, peeled

150g (5oz) cherry tomatoes

2 tablespoons olive oil

½ x 500g (1lb) packet ciabatta bread mix

50g (2oz) black olives, pitted and chopped

125g (4oz) feta cheese, crumbled

small handful of torn basil leaves

freshly ground black pepper

1 Preheat the oven to 220°C (fan oven 200°C), gas mark 7. Chop the aubergine, courgettes, peppers and onion into 1cm (½ inch) chunks and place in a roasting tin with the cherry tomatoes, in a single layer. Drizzle over the olive oil, season well with black pepper and roast for 25–30 minutes.

2 Meanwhile, make up the half quantity of ciabatta dough mix according to the packet instructions, using half the suggested quantity of water and adding the chopped black olives as you knead the dough. Set aside.

3 Transfer the roasted vegetables to a shallow, round non-stick baking tin or gratin dish, about 23cm (9 inches) in diameter. Roll out the olive dough to a round a little larger than the tin and place on top of the vegetables. Press the dough down well and to the side of the tin. Bake for 15–20 minutes.

4 Cool for a few minutes, then place a large serving plate over the tin, invert and carefully turn out the vegetable crust. Tap the tin to make sure all the vegetables come away. Scatter the feta and basil over the vegetables and cut into wedges to serve.

butternut barley risi

Barley is an interesting grain with a nutty texture, which is very under-rated in my opinion. It is easily digested and highly nutritious, providing a good source of fibre, calcium and protein. It works perfectly in this cross between a rich stew and a risotto, which is topped with roasted chunks of butternut squash to serve.

SERVES 4

125g (4oz) pearl barley, rinsed
1 large butternut squash, peeled and deseeded
2 tablespoons olive oil
1 large leek, trimmed and finely sliced
1 garlic clove, peeled and finely chopped
2 bay leaves
2 large strips of orange peel
1.2 litres (2 pints) vegetable stock
4 tablespoons chopped flat leaf parsley
freshly ground black pepper
freshly grated Parmesan cheese, to serve

1 Soak the pearl barley in cold water to cover for 30 minutes. Preheat the oven to 200°C (fan oven 180°C), gas mark 6.

2 Cut the butternut squash into 2.5 cm (1 inch) pieces, place on a large roasting tray, drizzle with 1 tablespoon of the olive oil and season with black pepper. Roast in the oven for 35–40 minutes until tender and slightly caramelised.

3 Meanwhile, heat the remaining olive oil in a large saucepan. Add the leek and garlic and steam-fry for 5 minutes until softened. Drain the pearl barley and add to the leek with the bay leaves, orange peel and stock. Bring to the boil and simmer gently for 30 minutes or until the barley is just tender.

4 Stir the parsley through the risi and season with black pepper. Ladle into warm bowls or soup plates and top with the roasted butternut and Parmesan to serve.

sweet vegetable and coconut green curry

This speedy vegetable curry has a wonderful creamy texture, as half-fat coconut milk is used as the stock. Tofu, or soya bean curd, is an important source of high quality protein, especially for vegetarians. Tofu also contains beneficial antioxidants, calcium and other essential minerals, plus B vitamins and vitamin E. Petit pois are a must in the freezer as they are such a useful standby and provide vitamin C, which helps the body to absorb iron.

SERVES 4

2 teaspoons olive oil
1 onion, peeled and finely chopped
2 1/2 tablespoons Thai green curry paste
3 medium sweet potatoes, peeled
400g can half-fat coconut milk
1 cinnamon stick
150g packet marinated tofu
200g (7oz) petit pois
2 tablespoons chopped coriander leaves

1 Heat the olive oil in a pan. Add the onion and steam-fry for 5 minutes, then stir in the curry paste and cook for 1 minute.

2 Meanwhile, cut the sweet potatoes into 2.5cm (1 inch) chunks. Add to the spiced onion and stir to coat evenly in the mixture. Pour in the coconut milk and 150ml (1/4 pint) water, and add the cinnamon stick. Bring to the boil, cover and simmer for 20 minutes.

3 Stir in the tofu and petit pois, and cook for a further 3 minutes. Scatter over the coriander and serve with Thai fragrant rice.

8 puddings

elderflower and fruit jellies

This refreshing fruity elderflower jelly, flavoured with raspberries and blueberries, is a delightful way of enjoying one of your five-a-day fruit and veg. Raspberries are a rich source of vitamin C, which helps the body to absorb iron and also helps improve the health of your skin. If preferred, substitute vegetarian gelatine and use according to the packet instructions, but note that this product may not achieve such a crystal clear set.

SERVES 4

7 tablespoons elderflower cordial, plus extra
* to drizzle*
11g sachet powdered gelatine
100g (3¹/₂oz) raspberries
100g (3¹/₂oz) blueberries

1   Dilute the elderflower cordial with 600ml (1 pint) cold water. Pour 4 tablespoons into a small pan, sprinkle over the gelatine and set aside for 10 minutes.

2   Divide the raspberries and blueberries between four wine glasses or tumblers.

3   Place the pan containing the softened gelatine over a very gentle heat and swirl the pan until the gelatine has completely dissolved; do not overheat. Gradually pour in the remaining diluted cordial, stirring well over a low heat.

4   Pour the elderflower jelly liquid into the glasses and chill in the refrigerator for 3 hours or until softly set. Just before serving, spoon over a little extra cordial.

meringue parfaits with pineapple and orange salad

Crushed meringues and toasted hazelnuts are folded into creamy fat-free Greek yogurt, a good source of calcium. The mixture is semi-frozen in ramekins to make parfaits, then turned out and served with a zingy, vitamin C-rich pineapple and orange salad.

SERVES 4

500g tub fat-free Greek yogurt

4 meringues, crumbled

65g (2¹/₂oz) blanched hazelnuts, toasted and
  chopped, plus extra to finish (optional)

FOR THE FRUIT SALAD:

1 small pineapple

3 large oranges

1 Line four 150ml (¼ pint) ramekins with cling film. Put the yogurt into a large bowl and gently fold in the meringues and chopped hazelnuts. Spoon the mixture into the prepared ramekins and freeze for 2¹/₂ hours or until semi-frozen.

2 With a sharp knife, cut away the skin from the pineapple, then cut into wedges and remove the core. Cut each wedge into thin slices lengthways.

3 Using a small sharp knife, peel the oranges, removing all white pith, then cut out the segments between the membranes. Toss the pineapple slices and orange segments together in a serving bowl.

4 Turn the semi-frozen parfaits out on to serving plates and remove the cling film. Scatter with toasted chopped hazelnuts if you wish and arrange a few pieces of the fruit alongside. Serve accompanied by the rest of the pineapple and orange salad.

apples and pears

Juicy, succulent, versatile and often under-rated, apples and pears feature in most fruit bowls and make delectable desserts. Apples are a great high-energy snack and a good source of vitamin C.

There are numerous varieties available, but for me certain apples sing out. The beautiful Cox's Orange Pippin, with its russet coloured skin, is a refreshing, crisp eating apple. When cooking, core this apple, but leave the skin on and you will find it holds its shape well. Granny Smith's have a crisp, sharp flavour with an unmistakable deep green colour. Gala and Pink Lady apples are sweet and juicy, perfect to round off a meal.

Pears at their peak of ripeness have a sublime, delicate flavour. Red Williams and Comice are juicy dessert pears, superb for juicing, and mashing for tiny children. Pears canned in natural juice are a useful standby – try blitzing with custard for a fruity sauce. Each of these pudding recipes serves 4.

▲ red berry pear soup

Peel 4 ripe pears, retaining the stalks. Put 300ml (½ pint) cranberry juice, 250ml (8fl oz) apple juice, pared rind and juice of ½ orange, 4 cloves, 1 cinnamon stick, 1 rosemary sprig and 50g (2oz) sugar in a wide saucepan. Heat gently to dissolve sugar, then add the pear halves. Bring to the boil and cover with greaseproof paper. Reduce heat and poach for 30–40 minutes until tender. Serve the pears warm or cold, with a little syrup. Add a dollop of fromage frais and crumbled meringue.

apple marmalade with thick cinnamon toasts

Place 4 halved, cored and chopped large Cox's apples in a pan with 125g (4oz) sliced, ready-to-eat dried apricots, the grated zest and juice of 2 large oranges, and 2 tbsp dark muscovado sugar. Cook over a medium heat for 12–15 minutes until the apples are soft and jammy. Split and toast 4 cinnamon bagels and serve with the warm apple marmalade.

vanilla pear custard

Drain a 415g can pears in natural juice, reserving half the juice. Pour a 500g carton of low-fat custard into a food processor. Add the pears with the reserved juice and 1 tsp vanilla extract. Blend until smooth and creamy. Serve chilled. (This quantity is sufficient to serve 6.)

pears with mocha fondue

Pour 150ml (¼ pint) semi-skimmed milk into a pan and add 100g (3½oz) chopped bitter dark chocolate. Place over a medium heat and stir until melted. Dissolve 1 tsp instant coffee in 1 tbsp boiling water. Stir into the chocolate mixture and simmer for 2 minutes. Serve the mocha sauce in small espresso cups or teacups with ripe pear wedges for dipping.

▲ apple and blackberry crunch

Place 6 peeled, cored and chopped large Cox's apples and 250g (9oz) blackberries in a shallow ovenproof dish. For the crumble, rub 25g (1oz) diced butter into 175g (6oz) plain white flour until the mix resembles crumbs. Stir in 50g (2oz) demerara sugar, 2 tbsp pumpkin seeds, 2 tbsp sunflower seeds and 2 tbsp orange juice. Scatter over the fruit with a little extra sugar. Bake at 200°C, gas 6 for 35–40 minutes.

roasted maple fruits

Nectarines, fresh figs and pears are roasted in maple syrup and wine for another interesting way to up your daily fruit intake. I like to serve them hot, with frozen vanilla yogurt or fromage frais.

SERVES 4

3 small nectarines, halved and stoned
3 ripe pears, peeled, quartered and cored
3 tablespoons maple syrup
3 tablespoons white wine or apple juice
4 fresh figs, halved
40g (1¹/₂oz) flaked almonds

1 Preheat the oven to 200°C (fan oven 180°C), gas mark 6. Cut the nectarines and pears into thick wedges and place in a small roasting tin.

2 Pour the maple syrup and wine or apple juice over the fruits, then toss well to coat evenly. Roast in the oven for 10 minutes.

3 Add the figs to the roasting tin and baste with the pan juices. Scatter the flaked almonds over the fruits and roast for a further 12–15 minutes until the fruit is glazed and the nuts are golden. Serve hot, with yogurt or fromage frais.

chocolate and prune mousse

Prunes are the secret ingredient in this low-fat mousse. Like other dried fruits, they are highly nutritious and naturally sweet – reducing the amount of sugar required in the recipe. Prunes are a good source of potassium, magnesium, iron and fibre, and contain antioxidants that may help to protect the body from disease.

SERVES 4–6

100g (3½oz) plain dark chocolate (preferably luxury Belgian)

175g (6oz) ready-to-eat prunes

2 tablespoons brandy (optional)

3 egg whites

1 tablespoon caster sugar

cocoa powder, to dust

1 Break up the chocolate and place in a heatproof bowl over a pan of hot water. Leave until melted, then stir until smooth and set aside to cool slightly.

2 Place the prunes in a saucepan and barely cover with 150ml (¼ pint) water. Simmer very gently, stirring occasionally, until very, very soft. Transfer the warm prunes and any remaining liquid to a blender or food processor, and add the brandy if using. Whiz to a smooth purée.

3 Beat the egg whites in a large clean bowl until stiff, then whisk in half of the sugar. Add the remaining sugar and beat until thick and glossy.

4 Stir the melted chocolate into the prune purée and beat together. Stir in a spoonful of the whisked egg whites to loosen the mixture, then carefully fold in the remaining egg whites.

5 Spoon the mousse into small espresso coffee cups or glasses and chill until required. Just before serving, dust with cocoa powder.

citrus almond cake with tropical fruit salsa

A cooked orange (skin and all) is puréed and incorporated into this cake mixture, to create a deliciously moist, citrusy cake, without butter or margarine. To serve, simply dust with icing sugar and accompany with a refreshing, vitamin C-rich, tropical fruit salsa.
Illustrated on previous page

SERVES 4

1 large orange, washed and quartered
oil, to brush tin
flour, to dust
3 eggs, beaten
50g (2oz) ground almonds
75g (3oz) instant polenta
1/2 teaspoon baking powder
125g (4oz) caster sugar
grated zest and juice of 1 lemon
icing sugar, to dust
FOR THE FRUIT SALSA:
2 kiwi fruit, peeled
1 small, ripe mango, peeled and cut away from
  the stone
1 nectarine, halved and stoned
grated zest and juice of 1/2 lime

1   Place the orange in a saucepan, add enough water to cover and bring to the boil. Lower the heat and simmer for 25–30 minutes.

2   Preheat the oven to 190°C (fan oven 170°C), gas mark 5. Lightly oil and flour an 18–20cm (7–8 inch) round cake tin.

3   Remove the orange from the pan and chop roughly, discarding the pips. Put the warm chopped orange into a food processor and blend until very smooth. Add the eggs, ground almonds, polenta, baking powder, sugar and lemon zest, and whiz briefly to combine.

4   Pour the cake mixture into the prepared tin and bake for 25 30 minutes until just firm. Let cool in the tin slightly, then using a fork, prick the top of the cake all over and spoon over the lemon juice.

5   For the fruit salsa, chop the fruits and toss together with the lime zest and juice. Dust the cake with icing sugar and serve cut into wedges, with the fruit salsa.

fruit salad platter with biscotti brittle

A stylish, fun way of enjoying more than one of your five-a-day fruit and veg. Packed with vitamin C and sprinkled with a satisfying crunch of biscotti, this dessert couldn't be easier. As an alternative, you can crumble brandy snaps over the fruit. Strawberries are an exceptional source of vitamin C, and high in pectin, a soluble fibre that helps reduce cholesterol levels in the body. They also have strong antioxidant properties.

SERVES 4

1 small ripe Galia melon
1 large ripe mango
2 large kiwi fruit, peeled
2 ripe nectarines, halved and stoned
225g (8oz) strawberries
juice of 1 orange
100g (3¹/₂oz) biscotti biscuits

1 Halve the melon and scoop out the seeds with a spoon, then cut away the rind. Thickly slice the melon flesh. Peel the mango and cut into chunks, slicing the flesh away from the stone. Quarter the kiwi fruit and nectarines.

2 Arrange all of the fruits attractively on a large platter. Cover with cling film and chill until ready to serve. Place the biscotti in a polythene bag and lightly crush with a rolling pin.

3 Just before serving, squeeze the orange juice over the chilled fruits. Scatter with the crushed biscotti and serve at once.

hot plum pudding

Bubbling, hot fresh plums nestle beneath a cinnamon-scented muffin topping in this real 'comfort food' pudding that is surprisingly low in fat and high in fibre. The topping is a cross between a crumble and a sponge, and complements the plums perfectly. Other stone fruit, such as apricots, peaches and nectarines, can be substituted for the plums.

SERVES 4

600g (1¼ lb) plums, halved and stoned

finely grated zest and juice of 1 orange

2 tablespoons light muscovado sugar, plus extra to sprinkle

150g (5oz) plain flour

2 teaspoons baking powder

½ teaspoon ground cinnamon

40g (1½oz) caster sugar

3 tablespoons milk

3 tablespoons natural yogurt

1 egg

15g (½oz) butter, melted

1   Preheat the oven to 180°C (fan oven 160°C), gas mark 4. Place the plums in a shallow ovenproof serving dish in a single layer. Drizzle with the orange juice and scatter over the muscovado sugar. Bake in the oven for 15 minutes.

2   Meanwhile, sift the flour, baking powder and cinnamon together into a bowl and stir in the caster sugar. Make a well in the centre.

3   In another bowl, whisk together the milk, yogurt, egg and melted butter. Add to the dry ingredients, together with the orange zest, and mix lightly until just combined.

4   Take the baking dish from the oven and dollop the muffin mix on top of the plums, in 8 large spoonfuls to create a rough cobbler effect. Sprinkle over a little muscovado sugar.

5   Return the dish to the oven and bake for a further 20–25 minutes or until the muffin topping is golden and cooked. Serve warm with Greek yogurt, fromage frais or custard.

apple and apricot filo pie

Filo pastry is much lower in fat than shortcrust, sweet or puff pastry. Here it envelopes naturally sweet dessert apples and dried apricots to make a crisp, light pie. Serve warm, with fromage frais or vanilla pear custard (page 177).

SERVES 4

4 Cox's or small dessert apples, cored and sliced
175g (6oz) ready-to-eat dried apricots, sliced
1/2 teaspoon ground cinnamon
40g (1 1/2oz) muscovado or soft brown sugar
grated zest of 1 lemon
squeeze of lemon juice
6 large sheets of filo pastry
2 tablespoons milk
15g (1/2oz) butter, melted
4 tablespoons thin honey

1 Preheat the oven to 190°C (fan oven 170°C), gas mark 5. Toss the apples, dried apricots, cinnamon, brown sugar, lemon zest and juice together in a large bowl. Set aside.

2 Fold one large sheet of filo pastry in half and lay on a non-stick baking sheet. Brush with a little milk. Cover with another folded sheet of filo and brush with milk. Scatter half of the apple and apricot mixture on top.

3 Cover with a further two sheets of folded filo, brushing each with milk, then scatter over the remaining apple mixture. Layer the remaining two sheets of filo on top, this time brushing with the melted butter.

4 Using a sharp knife, score the top layer of the pie in a diamond pattern. Bake in the oven for 40–45 minutes until the apples are cooked and the pastry is golden. Meanwhile, in a saucepan, heat the honey with 4 tablespoons water and simmer for 3 minutes. Set aside to cool slightly.

5 Spoon the honey syrup over the pie and return to the oven for 5 minutes to glaze. Allow the pie to cool slightly before cutting. Serve warm.

chocolate and raisin brownies

Low-fat cream cheese and naturally sweet raisins make these brownies quite moist. They taste very chocolatey, even though they are low in fat. Best eaten on the day of baking, either as a dessert with yogurt or fromage frais, or on their own as a treat.

MAKES 9

150g (5oz) low-fat soft cheese
140g (4¹/₂oz) muscovado sugar
40g (1¹/₂oz) cocoa powder, sifted
2 egg whites
1 teaspoon vanilla extract
1 tablespoon semi-skimmed milk
50g (2oz) plain flour
¹/₂ teaspoon baking powder
75g (3oz) raisins
icing sugar, to dust

1 Preheat the oven to 180°C (fan oven 160°C), gas mark 4. Line a 15cm (6 inch) square baking tin with baking parchment.

2 In a large bowl, combine the soft cheese with the sugar. Add the cocoa powder, egg whites, vanilla extract and milk. Beat well until the mixture is smooth.

3 Sift the flour and baking powder together over the mixture, then fold in lightly, together with the raisins. Spoon the mixture into the prepared tin and bake for 25 minutes until springy to the touch.

4 Remove from the oven and allow to cool in the tin. Cut into 9 squares and dust the brownies with icing sugar just before serving.

index

Acknowledgements
Firstly my very special thanks to Louise Wooldridge and Jacks Waters for their hard work and dedication, you girls are the best and both
deserve medals! I am also very grateful to Janet Illsley, my editor, for all her hard work and advice. Thanks to Gus Filgate, Silvana Franco,
Vanessa Courtier, Jane Campsie and Anna-Lisa Aldridge for the brilliant photography. Finally I have to thank Tim, my husband, for always
being a devoted taster with a huge appetite.